The Healthy Breakfast
COOKBOOK

The Healthy
Breakfast
COOKBOOK

Easy, Balanced Recipes for Busy Mornings

Shayna Telesmanic

ROCKRIDGE
PRESS

For general information on our other products and services or to obtain technical support, please contact our Customer Care Department within the United States at (866) 744-2665, or outside the United States at (510) 253-0500.

Rockridge Press publishes its books in a variety of electronic and print formats. Some content that appears in print may not be available in electronic books, and vice versa.

Interior and Cover Designer: Mando Daniel
Art Producer: Maura Boland
Editor: Britt Bogan
Production Editor: Andrew Yackira

Photography © Darren Muir
Food styling by Yolanda Muir
Author photo courtesy of © Gianna Cardella of RPM PR

ISBN: Print 978-1-64152-890-0 | eBook 978-1-64152-891-7

R0

To my husband, Chris. You endure the failures, praise the successes, and continue to encourage me along the way.

Contents

Introduction

In recent years, breakfast has become more aspirational than the staple meal it has always been. Beautiful breakfasts are everywhere on Instagram, avocado toast is now a part of popular culture, and brunch is a beacon of leisure. It seems like everyone is telling us to stop and smell the pancakes.

As a mother of two, most of my mornings entail washing, dressing, and feeding two little bodies while gathering everything they need for their day. I always make sure they're fed and prepped first, which means feeding and prepping myself last, if at all. Sometimes breakfast seems more like a luxury rather than the day's most important meal.

But here's the case for making breakfast aspirational (and why it's not just for Instagram influencers). I truly believe breakfast is the day's most important meal, not only because it helps to regulate insulin and increase brain function, but also because it sets the tone for the whole day. Eating a delicious, nutritionally balanced breakfast helps you feel like you've done something good for yourself—and that's worth waking up for.

Breakfast, in fact, has a lot of life lessons for us. Like the value of time: If I have to choose between sleep and making breakfast, sleep always wins. That's why I'm a big proponent of meal prepping and planning ahead. In this book, you'll find recipes to make whether you're planning ahead or scrambling the morning of. Breakfast also teaches us the value of collaboration: I often ask my children to help with the prep because their efforts help teach them where their food comes from and the effort, time, and energy it takes to make it. Being a part of the process helps them understand how to make healthy choices.

My love of breakfast has inspired me to write an entire book filled with breakfast recipes. In this book, you'll discover recipes to help master egg preparation, cook perfectly crisp bacon, and create exquisitely fluffy pancakes. You'll also tackle less traditional items like crêpes, shakshuka, and quinoa breakfast bowls. You'll find a range of breakfast meals—some are very healthy and others are a bit more indulgent—all with the goal of helping you discover balance and fall in love with mornings again. So, rise and shine—it's time to get cooking!

CHAPTER 1

Rise and Shine!

Breakfast is a crucial meal but often is overlooked or quickly bypassed because we are in a rush to get out the door and start our day. Our hurry often leaves us grabbing quick fixes, which usually means nutrient-deficient processed food. This doesn't have to be the case; you can start the day with a happy stomach and the fuel you need to make it to lunch, without sacrificing quality. With preparation and planning, a few good recipes, and these tips, you can have your breakfast and eat it, too.

Why Morning Matters

We all know first impressions are critical. In fact, the beginning of almost any endeavor often sets the tone and chances for success. Why would mealtime be any different? There are many reasons breakfast is the most important meal of the day, but the most significant is that your first meal is the beginning of your relationship with food—a relationship, I would argue, that is as important as any other in your life. It deserves your time, intention, and resources.

Whether we are breaking our fast from the previous night or taking a break in the middle of our day, every time we eat is a chance to nourish and fuel our bodies. Food has the ability to affect our mood, ability to concentrate, energy level, and performance throughout the day.

Scientific research on eating breakfast illustrates that a variety of health benefits stem from a healthy morning meal. For example, eating within two hours of waking has a positive effect on sugar levels and insulin regulation, thereby reducing the risk of diabetes and the negative effects associated with insulin dysregulation. Meta-analysis has also demonstrated that eating breakfast regularly can reduce the risk of heart disease, because people who eat a healthy breakfast have a decreased risk of weight gain from overeating throughout the rest of the day. Fueling your body and brain at the start of the day also sets you up for higher productivity and a better attitude to take on the challenges that the day can bring.

MORNINGS AROUND THE WORLD

The recipes here have an obvious Western bent, so let's take a moment to explore breakfast traditions from around the world.

In countries like Spain, Italy, and France, that place a heavy emphasis on the midday meal, a large "traditional" breakfast is rare. They rely on a strong espresso, possibly with steamed milk, and a plain or savory bread roll. Meanwhile, in England where the midday meal does not reign supreme, a typical breakfast includes eggs, bacon, sausage, and beans. In Germany, where hearty breakfasts also reign supreme, you may find a spread of cured meats and cheeses.

In Asian countries, the breakfast menu looks quite similar to the dinner one. Korean restaurants are just as busy for the morning rush as they are for dinner. Japanese families start the day with fish, rice, pickled vegetables, and even miso soup.

Breakfast in South America tends to be light and protein-filled to provide enough energy to last until the big midday meal. A typical Brazilian breakfast, for example, usually involves a variation of ham, cheese, and bread, served up with strong black coffee.

A Balanced Breakfast

Wherever you are in the world, whatever tradition or cultural influences the components of your first meal of the day, the critical common element is balance. Your first meal each day should be balanced and nutritious, made with whole foods and fresh ingredients . . . and, of course, still taste delicious.

Attaining balance in any aspect of life can be a challenge. When it comes to a balanced diet and your nutritional needs, consider the three main macronutrients. These are the fundamental building blocks of the food we eat:

protein, fat, and carbohydrates (in the form of fiber). If you can just remember to include these three items at each meal, you will have set the foundation for a healthy, balanced diet. Keep in mind, however, that your diet must also include micronutrients. These are vitamins and minerals that are found in food. Let's break it all down so you can understand why each is important and how you can consume them.

Packed with Protein

Proteins, which are actually made up of smaller molecules called amino acids, are the building blocks of our organs, skin, and muscles. They also facilitate the production of hormones, enzymes, and antibodies. Studies have shown that eating protein helps to build muscle mass as well as decrease belly fat. It is also linked to lowering blood pressure and controlling diabetes.

Not all protein is equal though. It is important to choose high-quality protein. When deciding which protein to consume, animal protein, like chicken, beef, and fish, is often the obvious choice, and there are plenty of other healthy alternatives. Protein can also come out of nuts, seeds, beans, soy, eggs, oats, and Greek yogurt. High-quality protein, also known as a complete protein, means that it contains all necessary amino acids that our bodies require. It also refers to bioavailability, or how easily our bodies can digest the proteins to utilize the energy as fuel.

Carbohydrates that Count

Carbohydrates, or "carbs" for short, are present in food in the form of fiber, starch, and sugar. The most common examples that come to mind are breads and pastas. In balance with the other macronutrients, carbs are integral in properly fueling our bodies. Everything from our muscles to our brains uses some form of sugar as fuel, and this sugar predominately comes from carbohydrates.

Yet like proteins, not all carbs are created equal. It is important to consume whole carbs, or those that have not had the fiber stripped out while being processed. Carbohydrates are, after all, the best source of fiber. The best sources of whole carbohydrates are whole grains, vegetables, legumes, and whole fruit. The foods that give carbs a bad name, the "empty" carbs like highly processed cereal, white bread, juice, prepackaged muffins, and flavored yogurts, spike blood sugar and should be eaten sparingly.

Healthy Fats

Fat in foods has long been a point of contention. Up until recently, the trend was toward low-fat diets. These days, however, the research suggests that fat isn't as dangerous to our health as we once thought. We all need fat in our diets, and it is nothing to be scared of. In fact, essential fatty acids are considered "essential" for a reason; in part, they regulate hormone production, ensure proper thyroid function, and regulate blood pressure, liver function, and our immune system, as well as support healthy skin and nails. Essential fatty acids must come from our diets because our bodies can't produce them on their own. Omega-3 fatty acids are one of the best types of polyunsaturated fat, and can be found in many foods. For example, fish; seeds (like pumpkin, chia, and flax); walnuts; eggs; and soybean products like tofu and tempeh are all good sources of omega-3 fatty acids.

"Good fat" usually refers to unsaturated fat. These fats are typically liquid at room temperature and are more easily broken down by the body without raising cholesterol levels in unhealthy ways. Unsaturated fat provides flavor in food, helps satiate our hunger, and may even help with weight loss. Then there are saturated fats, which generally aren't as healthy. They may taste good but can be linked to increasing cholesterol levels and heart disease. One major problem with saturated fat is that it is often consumed with sugar, which together causes weight gain and the many problems that stem from it. The fat that truly gives fat a bad name is trans-fat, the fat to avoid. This is often found in fried, fast, and processed foods like packaged snack items, baked goods, and hydrogenated cooking oils.

Vitamins and Minerals

While it is important that we get our three macronutrients, our daily intake of micronutrients is equally important. These micronutrients include essential vitamins and minerals found in food, such as calcium, magnesium, potassium, fiber, and vitamins A, C, D, and E. They are responsible for performing millions of jobs in our body, like bolstering our immune system, repairing cells, converting food into energy, and strengthening our bones, to name a few.

Studies reveal that nearly half of Americans routinely take multivitamin dietary supplements. Nevertheless, studies also show that these supplements do not provide as much benefit to overall health as eating real food rich in vitamins and minerals does.

BACON, DONUTS, WAFFLES—OH MY!

When you think of breakfast, do visions of pancakes, donuts, and waffles pop into your head? These delicious treats are the breakfast's desserts. They can be a special treat enjoyed on occasion, but, on a regular basis, it is wiser not to start the day with foods that are high in sugar and low in nutritional density. These foods will spike your insulin levels and provide you a rush of energy, but will also cause a mid-morning crash before you reach lunch.

Good news though. You can still enjoy these delightful treats if you choose wisely or make a few simple swaps. And by all means, on occasion, opt for the full-fledged donut and enjoy every single bite without remorse.

Use this book as a guide to make a few simple swaps for the foods that we have a hard time turning down.

- **Pancakes and waffles.** Make delicious, protein-filled pancakes by mixing in peanut butter or protein powders, or use alternative flours like almond flour (see Protein-Packed Banana Pancakes, page 91). When topping pancakes and waffles, be sure to use real maple syrup rather than the processed stuff made with high-fructose corn syrup. Real maple syrup provides nutrients like zinc, magnesium, and potassium, but it still very sugary, so pour it sparingly. You can also top pancakes with fruit, peanut butter, or a homemade compote (see Seasonal Fruit Compote, page 28). Cut down on sugar intake by making fresh-squeezed juice instead of store-bought juice.

- **Bagels and cream cheese.** Bagels can be more calorie- and carbohydrate-packed than donuts. They can still be a good breakfast option though if you choose a whole-grain bagel and top it with nutrient-dense spreads like hummus, avocado, and eggs.

- **Store-bought flavored yogurt and granola.** Store-bought yogurt, especially with fruit, can contain a lot of hidden sugar. Plain Greek or Icelandic yogurt sweetened only with vanilla, fresh fruit, or granola you've made yourself (see Homemade Granola, page 32) is a healthier option.

Healthy Made Easy

Making a healthy breakfast for an entire family or even for yourself can feel like a full-time job, especially when paired with getting ready for the day. It may seem like healthy dishes using whole, fresh ingredients, rather than processed, grab-and-go items, require more effort. To set yourself up for success, like with anything, it is best to plan ahead. Many of the recipes in this book are great make-ahead options that can either be quickly assembled in the morning or grabbed out of the refrigerator on the way out the door. So, you can enjoy the grab-and-go convenience but with all of the healthy benefits of a home-cooked meal.

Plan ahead. The old adage "if you fail to plan, you plan to fail" rings true here. Plan out your morning meals. This is the most foolproof way to ensure that you're getting a healthy, tasty breakfast in the morning because it is one less decision you have to make upon first waking.

Prepare the night before. While cooking dinner, chop any items that you need for the following morning. Or even set out a few things you'll need in the morning (frying pan, spatula, plates) could make the morning meal prep go a bit more smoothly.

Cook in bulk. Making staple breakfast items like granola or egg muffins in larger quantities will help make meal prep even faster. In this book, you'll find plenty of recipes that are great make-ahead options.

Keep it simple. Sometimes we just don't have time to plan ahead. On mornings when you need a quick solution, keep it simple by choosing things that you can throw together like a delicious lox wrap or creative toast combination. On these mornings, pick out a recipe that takes 10 minutes or less—these are the recipes in this book labeled **"Super-rushed"** and they are for you, my kindred spirits!

Develop a routine. Morning rituals make for an easy transition into the day. If you can develop a daily habit that starts your day off right, this routine will help ensure an overall healthy lifestyle. Some examples include starting the day by drinking a glass of water, doing a few simple stretches, and practicing mindful breathing or meditation before breakfast.

FINALLY, THE PERFECT
BOILED EGGS

Hard-boiled eggs can be a finicky thing to make. No two eggs are the same, so boiling them always yields varying results. I have found that utilizing the Instant Pot to make a batch of hard-boiled eggs is the best, most fool-proof method. It takes about 20 minutes in total. It takes five minutes to come to pressure. I cook on high pressure for five minutes (for a true hard-boiled egg), and allow for five minutes of natural release, followed by a five-minute ice water bath. The peel will slip right off the egg, like a jacket on a warm summer day.

If you don't have an Instant Pot, you can achieve the same result with a sauce-pot and good fitting lid. Start by placing eggs straight out of the refrigerator into the sauce pot and fill with cool water, covering an inch over the eggs. Put the uncovered pot on the stove and bring to a boil. Once a rolling boil is achieved, cover the pot and remove it from the heat. The time you allow it to sit will determine the type of center.

- Slightly runny, soft-boiled eggs: 4 minutes

- Custard like, firm soft-boiled eggs: 6 minutes

- Firm yet creamy hard-boiled eggs: 10 minutes

- Very firm hard-boiled eggs: 12 minutes

After cooking for desired time, remove eggs from water with a slotted spoon and soak for 5 minutes in an ice bath. Then peel.

Tools to Take on the Morning

Making healthy breakfasts requires basic kitchen items like pots, pans, baking dishes, and sheet pans or baking sheets. A few other items that will make your life easier when it comes to making breakfast include:

Muffin tin. A muffin tin can be your best breakfast mate. Not only can you can bake delicious muffins, but you can also poach an egg. Most casseroles can be cooked in a muffin tin to reduce the bake time, as well as make perfect single-serve portions.

Blender. There is nothing better than a powerful blender for making a killer smoothie, but it can also take the place of a juicer. You can use it to whip a sauce or pancake batter as well as get adventurous to grind up your own flour alternative or nut butter.

Mason jars. Finally a reason to hoard and reuse mason jars. Many breakfast items, like overnight oats, yogurt parfaits, and even egg dishes, can be prepared in advance and stored in jars.

Baking sheet liners. It is best to cover your baking sheet with parchment paper or a reusable silicone baking mat. This makes it easier to clean up messes and keep your baking sheets in top condition.

Cast-iron skillet. A well-seasoned cast-iron skillet is like a cook's bestie. It takes time and attention to develop a good relationship, but once you put in the work, it makes life so much easier. This nonstick surface is so versatile, you can start a dish on the stove and finish it in the oven. Plus, the surface can endure use by any utensil, from a wooden spoon to a metal spatula.

Instant Pot (nice to have). An Instant Pot, along with a coffee machine, has permanent residence on my kitchen counter because of its versatility and usefulness. It is easy to whip up the best hard-boiled eggs but you can also use the slow cooker function.

Waffle maker (nice to have). To craft fluffy, customized waffles, it is lovely, but not critical, to have a waffle maker.

Ingredients to Keep on Hand

There are some items that you should keep on hand to make meal prep easier.

Pantry

- Nuts and seeds, such as cashews, almonds, macadamia, pecan, flaxseed, chia
- Nut butter(s), such as almond, peanut, cashew, sesame seed
- Breakfast-friendly grains like rolled oats, quinoa, polenta, grits
- Shelf-stable milks like coconut, almond, oat
- Baking goods, such as flour, baking powder, baking soda
- Sliced bread: healthiest options include sprouted whole wheat, sour dough, flax bread, sprouted rye, and 100% whole wheat
- Avocado
- Sweet potatoes
- Canned (or dried) beans
- Canned tomatoes
- Cacao powder
- Shredded coconut
- Ghee
- MCT and/or coconut oil
- Chicken broth
- Olive oil
- Local honey
- Real maple syrup
- Cinnamon
- Spices like cumin, chili powder, garlic powder, paprika
- Sea salt
- Pepper

Fridge

- Organic eggs
- Milk of your choice
- Grass-fed butter
- Fresh berries
- Tomatoes
- Cottage cheese
- Sour cream
- Greek yogurt
- Vegetables, such as kale, spinach, Brussels sprouts, peppers
- Cooked lentils
- Smoked salmon
- Bacon, low sodium, nitrate- and sugar-free
- Tortillas
- Salsa
- Cheese, like Parmesan, goat, Cheddar

Freezer

- Frozen fruit/ vegetables
- Peeled frozen bananas for smoothies

Eat Your Greens Smoothie, *Page 13*

CHAPTER 2

Smoothies and Drinks

Do you like to start the day with a warm cup of coffee or tea? Breakfast is not just for food; there are numerous beverages that will also kick-start your day. Whether you whip up a smoothie or try a juice recipe, these high-fiber refreshments pack the necessary nutrients. If you prefer a warm cup of joe but are trying to limit caffeine intake, try the Warm Golden Milk (page 17) or Matcha Latte (page 18).

Base Smoothie Formula

Smoothies provide a great start to your day because you can fill them with protein, fat, and fiber and put your best nutritional foot forward. For the base smoothie, you'll need greens (such as celery, chard, kale, or spinach), fruit (apple, avocado, banana, berries, peach, or pineapple), liquid (juice, milk, nondairy milk, or water), and a fat or protein (nut butter, protein powder, chia seeds, flaxseed). If you adhere to this basic formula when making smoothies, you can customize each for flavor, availability, and diet. SERVES 2

DAIRY FREE

GLUTEN FREE

VEGAN

SUPER-RUSHED

PREP TIME: 5 MINUTES

2 cups greens of choice

1 cup fruit

½ cup base liquid

¼ cup fat or protein, such as nut butter or protein powder (see ingredient tip)

½ cup ice, if needed

In a blender, layer the greens first so the heavier fruit will push them down into the blade to make sure they are well blended. Then add the fruit, liquid, nut butter, and ice. Blend until smooth and combined.

THE NIGHT BEFORE

To save time in the morning, place items like greens and fruit in the freezer. In the morning, pour the contents of the bag into the blender, add the liquid, ice, and fat or protein, and blend.

INGREDIENT TIP

In addition to the nut butter, use any combination of flaxseed, nut butter, cinnamon, protein power, chia seeds, or spirulina to supercharge your smoothie with flavor and protein.

Per serving: Calories: 298; Fat: 22g; Protein: 12g; Carbohydrates: 21g; Fiber: 8g; Sodium: 312mg; Sugar: 6g

Eat Your Greens Smoothie

It's not always easy to eat all your veggies throughout the day. So, why not blend up a day's worth and get them all in at one meal? This high-fiber, low-calorie smoothie will make it easy for you to eat the rainbow. The frozen banana is key to a creamy finish, and the pineapple provides a subtle sweetness so it doesn't feel like you're just eating a blended salad. SERVES 2

DAIRY FREE
GLUTEN FREE
VEGAN
SUPER-RUSHED

PREP TIME: 5 MINUTES

2 cups torn, stemmed kale
   or spinach leaves
1 celery stalk,
   roughly chopped
1 carrot, roughly chopped
½ apple, chopped
½ cup chopped pineapple
½ avocado
1 frozen banana, peeled
½ cup coconut water
½ cup pineapple juice
½ cup ice, as needed

In a blender, layer the spinach first, so the pressure of the other ingredients pushes it into the blade to make sure it is well blended. Then add the celery, carrot, apple, pineapple, avocado, banana, coconut water, pineapple juice, and ice, as needed. Blend until smooth and combined.

MAKE IT SWEETER

The pineapple juice provides sweetness here; add more if it's not sweet enough for you. You can also sweeten with a bit of agave nectar.

INGREDIENT TIP

Before a banana goes bad, peel it and store it in an airtight container or bag in the freezer.

Per Serving: Calories: 266; Fat: 7g; Protein: 5g; Carbohydrates: 51g; Fiber: 9g; Sodium: 126mg; Sugar: 27g

Funky Monkey Smoothie

This is a well-rounded choice for a breakfast meal. It reminds me of a peanut butter cup and is sure to satisfy any sweet tooth. Made with pure cacao powder, it is high in antioxidants and delivers protein from spinach and healthy fats from the almond butter. Freeze 2 bananas the night before. SERVES 2

DAIRY FREE

GLUTEN FREE

VEGAN

SUPER-RUSHED

PREP TIME: 5 MINUTES

1 cup fresh spinach

2 frozen bananas, peeled

½ cup ice

½ cup almond milk or
   coconut milk

¼ cup cacao powder

¼ cup almond butter

In a blender, layer the spinach first, so the pressure of the other ingredients pushes it into the blade to make sure it is well blended. Then add the bananas, ice, almond milk, cacao powder, and almond butter. Blend until smooth and combined.

MAKE IT HEALTHIER

Use cacao powder, not **cocoa** powder. *Cacao* powder contains antioxidants whereas cocoa powder often has added sugar and palm oil. If the recipe is not sweet enough for you, add 2 to 4 dried pitted dates or ¼ cup of fresh strawberries.

Per Serving: Calories: 346; Fat: 22g; Protein: 9g; Carbohydrates: 41g; Fiber: 8g; Sodium: 204mg; Sugar: 17g

Tropical Smoothie Bowl

If you like Piña Coladas, this tropical smoothie will float your boat. The bright pineapple and subtle coconut flavors will call up images of soft sands and warm waters—plus it's packed with protein and fiber. You may be used to drinking your smoothies, but it is easier to view it as a meal when eating it with a spoon. **SERVES 1**

DAIRY FREE

GLUTEN FREE

VEGAN

SUPER-RUSHED

PREP TIME: 5 MINUTES

For the base

1 banana

1 cup pineapple chunks

¼ cup unsweetened
   coconut flakes or chunks

½ cup coconut water

¼ cup coconut milk

½ cup ice, if needed

For the toppings

2 strawberries, sliced

½ kiwi, chopped

1 tablespoon coconut flakes

1 tablespoon chia seeds

1 tablespoon sliced almonds

To make the base

In a blender, combine the banana, pineapple, coconut flakes, coconut water, coconut milk, and ice, as needed (if using frozen fruit, you should not need the ice). Blend until smooth and combined.

To add the toppings

Pour the smoothie into a bowl. Layer the strawberries, kiwi, coconut flakes, chia seeds, and almonds and serve with a spoon.

Per Serving: Calories: 530; Fat: 29g; Protein: 8g; Carbohydrates: 70g; Fiber: 16g; Sodium: 20mg; Sugar: 39g

Keto Coffee Smoothie

Your morning coffee habit might be a place for sugars and saturated fats to sneak in. This high-fat smoothie satiates your hunger and provides sustained energy for the morning ahead. The ghee, instead of regular butter, produces a smoother smoothie. SERVES 2

GLUTEN FREE
VEGETARIAN
SUPER-RUSHED

PREP TIME: 3 MINUTES

1 frozen banana, peeled

½ cup ice

1 cup cold-brew coffee

1½ teaspoons coconut oil

1 teaspoon grass-fed ghee

In a blender, combine the banana, ice, coffee, coconut oil, and ghee. Blend until smooth and combined.

MAKE IT SWEET

The banana should add plenty of sweetness, but if you prefer your coffee even sweeter, add a few drops of agave nectar or pure maple syrup.

Per Serving: Calories: 142; Fat: 11g; Protein: 1g; Carbohydrates: 14g; Fiber: 2g; Sodium: 1mg; Sugar: 7g

Warm Golden Milk

Drinking a cup of this creamy liquid gold beverage is a daily habit for many renowned health food enthusiasts. Turmeric is an anti-inflammatory that aids digestion, and ginger calms the stomach and is believed to help reduce anxiety. Pairing black pepper with turmeric gives the golden spice a super boost of antioxidant, anti-inflammatory, and disease-fighting qualities. The capsaicin in black pepper, with health-boosting qualities of its own, helps with the absorption of turmeric. I suggest trying the recipe without sweetening it and adding maple syrup, a drop at a time, if needed. SERVES 2

DAIRY FREE

GLUTEN FREE

VEGAN

SUPER-RUSHED

PREP TIME: 1 MINUTE

COOK TIME: 5 MINUTES

¾ cup canned coconut milk

¾ cup unsweetened
   almond milk

1 teaspoon turmeric powder

½ teaspoon cinnamon

¼ teaspoon ginger

Pinch of black pepper

Pure maple syrup

In a small saucepan over medium heat, stir together the coconut milk, almond milk, turmeric, cinnamon, ginger, and pepper. Cook for about 5 minutes, stirring, or until warm. Pour into a mug, and sweeten with maple syrup, to taste.

Per Serving: Calories: 233; Fat: 21g; Protein: 2g; Carbohydrates: 6g; Fiber: 3g; Sodium: 45mg; Sugar: 4g

Matcha Latte

Matcha means "powdered tea," and this green one is the Hulk of morning beverages. It is full of antioxidants, contains caffeine, and is thought to speed up your metabolism, regulate blood sugar, and provide anti-aging benefits. Matcha is traditionally prepared using a bamboo whisk to mix the powdered tea with boiling water while you take a few moments to meditate. As you make your morning cup, say a few positive affirmations to start your day with a good mind-set. SERVES 1

DAIRY FREE

GLUTEN FREE

VEGETARIAN

LESS THAN 5 INGREDIENTS

SUPER-RUSHED

PREP TIME: 3 MINUTES

COOK TIME: 5 MINUTES

1 teaspoon ceremonial
    grade matcha green
    tea powder

⅓ cup water

1 cup whole milk

1 teaspoon local honey
    (optional)

1. Put the matcha in a mug and set aside.

2. In a small saucepan over medium-high heat, heat the water until it is hot but not boiling. Slowly pour the hot water over the matcha and, using a small whisk (bamboo or otherwise), incorporate the tea into the water until it is no longer lumpy. This takes about 2 minutes.

3. Return the saucepan to medium heat and warm the milk, whisking continuously. Whisk in the matcha mixture and heat until it reaches your desired temperature. Serve with honey to sweeten (if using).

COOKING HACK

If you like your milk frothy but do not have a milk frother, after heating the milk and stirring in the tea, use an immersion blender to blend until frothy.

Per Serving: Calories: 149; Fat: 7g; Protein: 8g; Carbohydrates: 11g; Fiber: 1g; Sodium: 86mg; Sugar: 11g

Ginger Carrot Juice

Toss out that old carton of OJ and replace it with fresh veggies and ginger. Push all the ingredients through a juicer and make a large batch for the week ahead. You can easily double or triple the recipe to keep in the refrigerator. Consider saving leftover pulp to make delicious High-Fiber Carrot Cake Muffins (page 104). No juicer? No problem. See the following cooking hack. **SERVES 2**

DAIRY FREE

GLUTEN FREE

VEGAN

LESS THAN 5 INGREDIENTS

SUPER-RUSHED

PREP TIME: 5 MINUTES

2 oranges, peeled

2 carrots, halved

1 large apple, quartered

1 tablespoon grated, peeled
  fresh ginger

Push the oranges, carrots, apple, and ginger through a juicer. Pour the liquid into a pitcher and refrigerate to chill, or serve immediately.

COOKING HACK

If you do not have a juicer, roughly chop the apple and carrots, slice the fresh ginger, and juice the oranges. Put the ingredients in a blender and blend until smooth. Set a fine-mesh sieve or colander over a medium bowl and pour the contents from the blender through it. Use a spatula to push the liquid into the bowl. Pour the liquid into cups or a pitcher.

Per Serving: Calories: 84; Fat: 0g; Protein: 2g; Carbohydrates: 26g; Fiber: 2g; Sodium: 30mg; Sugar: 18g

Infused Water

After fasting all night, your body needs hydration. It's great to get into the habit of drinking a big glass of water in the morning, but sometimes it's hard. Why not trick your taste buds with a delicious infusion of fruits, veggies, and herbs? It's a great way to hydrate while introducing vitamins, minerals, and antioxidants. Once you get the hang of it, the flavor combinations are endless. Here are a few of my favorites. SERVES 4

DAIRY FREE

GLUTEN FREE

VEGAN

LESS THAN 5 INGREDIENTS

PREP TIME: 5 MINUTES

CHILL TIME: 1 HOUR

For the strawberry basil infusion

1 cup sliced strawberries

½ cup fresh basil

4 cups water

For the cucumber mint infusion

1 cup sliced cucumber

½ cup fresh mint

1 lemon, sliced

4 cups water

For the tropical infusion

1 orange, sliced

1 cup cubed pineapple

1 cup sliced strawberries

4 cups water

To make the strawberry basil infusion

In a pitcher, combine the strawberries and basil. Add the water and refrigerate for 1 hour to chill, or up to overnight. This will keep, refrigerated, for up to 5 days.

To make the cucumber mint infusion

In a pitcher, combine the cucumber, mint, and lemon. Add the water and refrigerate for 1 hour to chill, or up to overnight. This will keep, refrigerated, for up to 5 days.

To make the tropical infusion

In a pitcher, combine the orange, pineapple, and strawberries. Add the water and refrigerate for 1 hour to chill, or up to overnight. This will keep, refrigerated, for up to 5 days.

THE NIGHT BEFORE

Make travel versions in mason jars, cover the jars, and refrigerate. The longer it soaks, the more intense the flavors will be.

Per Serving: Calories: 0; Fat: 0g; Protein: 0g; Carbohydrates: 0g; Fiber: 0g; Sodium: 0mg; Sugar: 0g

Pineapple Basil Cooler

Pineapple is a metabolism booster that strengthens the immune system. This drink pairs pineapple with coconut water, which is known for replacing key electrolytes, thereby creating a thirst-quenching superstar beverage that delivers important vitamins and nutrients. Consider this your new sports drink, only without the processed sugar. And don't be afraid to try other flavor combos like cucumber and cilantro; mint and lemon; or beet, lemon, and ginger. SERVES 2

DAIRY FREE

GLUTEN FREE

VEGAN

LESS THAN 5 INGREDIENTS

SUPER-RUSHED

PREP TIME: 5 MINUTES

½ cup pineapple juice (not from concentrate), chilled

½ cup coconut water, chilled

½ cup fresh basil leaves

In a blender, combine the pineapple juice, coconut water, and basil. Blend until whipped.

LOVE YOUR LEFTOVERS

Make a larger batch to keep in the refrigerator to enjoy later. Shake or stir to mix the flavors again before serving.

Per Serving: Calories: 37; Fat: 0g; Protein: 1g; Carbohydrates: 9g; Fiber: 1g; Sodium: 33mg; Sugar: 7g

Apple Crumble, *Page 29*

CHAPTER 3

Yogurt and Fruit

Yogurt is one of the oldest and most popular fermented foods enjoyed around the world. Made of fermented milk, yogurt contains live bacteria to help with digestion and gut health. It is also a great source of calcium. Check out how to make your own homemade version (see page 24) and use it to top other breakfast dishes like Chia Seed Pudding (see page 25), Greek Yogurt Banana Split (see page 27), and Apple Crumble (see page 29).

Homemade Yogurt

Although yogurt is believed to be a good part of a healthy diet, it is important to pay attention to the sugar content of store-bought brands and limit versions with fruit mix-ins. Replace those options with plain Greek yogurt or, even better, this home-made version. Yogurt contains *lactobacillus acidophilus*, an important bacterium that promotes gut health, which some consider a cornerstone of our overall health and well-being. SERVES 4

GLUTEN FREE

VEGETARIAN

LESS THAN 5 INGREDIENTS

PREP TIME: 2 MINUTES

COOK TIME: 16 MINUTES

FERMENTING TIME:

6 HOURS

CHILL TIME: 4 HOURS

2 cups whole milk

½ cup plain yogurt

1. In a small saucepan over medium heat, heat the milk for about 6 minutes, or until the temperature reaches 180°F. Remove from the heat and let cool to 110°F. To help speed this process, fill a baking dish with ice water and put the pan in it. Stir the milk for 7 to 10 minutes so it cools evenly.

2. Transfer half the warmed milk into a small bowl and whisk in the yogurt until smooth. (After you create your first batch of homemade yogurt, you can use your own yogurt for this step.) Stir the yogurt mixture back into the warmed milk. Put a lid on the saucepan and put it in a warm place, like the oven with the light on, for 6 hours until the yogurt sets. The longer it sits, the tarter and thicker it will become. (If you need the pan for something else, transfer the yogurt into a shallow dish with a lid.)

3. Let cool, then refrigerate for 4 hours to chill.

MAKE IT SWEET

To sweeten the yogurt, stir in honey to taste until fully combined. You can also add a few drops of freshly squeezed lemon juice or vanilla extract to enhance the flavor of the yogurt or reduce the tartness.

Per Serving: Calories: 95; Fat: 4g; Protein: 6g; Carbohydrates: 8g; Fiber: 0g; Sodium: 70mg; Sugar: 8g

Chia Seed Pudding

This recipe is prepped the evening before and will keep in the refrigerator for up to seven days, so you can make a week's worth and take it to go. Chia seeds pack fiber and omega-3 fatty acids, but it's important to watch the sugar content of pre-made puddings. Make your own pudding and pair it with a protein, such as sliced almonds or flaxseed, to ensure that this breakfast treat delivers its well-rounded nutrient-dense best. SERVES 1

DAIRY FREE

GLUTEN FREE

VEGETARIAN

LESS THAN 5 INGREDIENTS

PREP TIME: 5 MINUTES

SET TIME: 6 HOURS, OR
UP TO OVERNIGHT

½ cup coconut milk, or
   almond milk

2 tablespoons chia seeds

1 teaspoon local honey
   (optional)

1. In an 8-ounce mason jar, stir together the coconut milk, chia seeds, and honey (if using) until well mixed. Let settle for 2 minutes and stir again. Cover and refrigerate for a minimum of 6 hours, or up to overnight.

2. Sprinkle on your favorite toppings and enjoy.

MAKE IT YOUR OWN

This recipe is easily tailored to your tastes. Add toppings such as strawberries, blueberries, coconut flakes, almond butter, or cacao nibs to name a few.
Try Homemade Granola (page 32) or Seasonal Fruit Compote (page 28) for homemade flavor boosters.

Per Serving: Calories: 158; Fat: 10g; Protein: 5g; Carbohydrates: 13g; Fiber: 9g; Sodium: 95mg; Sugar: 1g

Fruit and Yogurt Parfait with Homemade Granola

"Parfait" means perfect. Build your own perfect breakfast parfait with colorful layers of fruit and Greek yogurt for added protein. If you make it instead of grabbing one at the store, you can reduce your sugar intake. Try making one or two in advance in small mason jars to have ready to grab and go on busy mornings. **SERVES 1**

GLUTEN FREE
VEGETARIAN
LESS THAN 5 INGREDIENTS
SUPER-RUSHED

PREP TIME: 10 MINUTES

6 ounces Homemade Yogurt
(page 24), or store-bought
plain Greek yogurt

½ cup chopped fresh fruit,
such as strawberries,
peaches, blueberries,
raspberries, apples

2 tablespoons Homemade
Granola (page 32), or
store-bought granola

1 teaspoon local honey,
or pure maple syrup
(optional)

1. In a small mason jar or cup, put half the yogurt.

2. Add half the fruit, followed by the remaining yogurt.

3. Top with remaining fruit. Sprinkle with the granola and honey (if using).

THE NIGHT BEFORE

Assemble and refrigerate the night before, but add the granola just before eating so it doesn't become soggy.

Per Serving: Calories: 199; Fat: 10g; Protein: 17g; Carbohydrates: 34g; Fiber: 4g; Sodium: 84mg; Sugar: 21g

Greek Yogurt Banana Split

Starting the day with a little "dessert" is sure to put a smile on your face. Bananas are low on the glycemic index and are a great choice for sustained energy. In this "banana split," you will replace ice cream with Greek yogurt and drizzle on nut butter and nutrient-dense toppings. **SERVES 1**

GLUTEN FREE

VEGETARIAN

SUPER-RUSHED

PREP TIME: 5 MINUTES

1 banana, halved lengthwise

¼ cup vanilla Greek yogurt

2 tablespoons almond butter

¼ cup sliced strawberries

⅓ cup Homemade Granola (page 32), or store-bought granola

1. Put the banana halves in a shallow bowl.

2. Spoon the Greek yogurt into the bowl and drizzle it with almond butter. If the almond butter is too thick to drizzle, heat it for 15 seconds in the microwave.

3. Top with the strawberries and granola.

MAKE IT TO YOUR TASTE

Play around with different toppings, like dried fruit and nuts, or switch out the banana for thin apple slices and make "apple nachos."

Per Serving: Calories: 621; Fat: 30g; Protein: 19g; Carbohydrates: 80g; Fiber: 9g; Sodium: 35mg; Sugar: 34g

Seasonal Fruit Compote

Compote is made by simmering fresh or frozen fruit in a bit of naturally sweet juice. This combination is high in antioxidants and is great on top of yogurt, oatmeal, pancakes, waffles, or even toast. By making it yourself, you control and can reduce the sugar content. SERVES 4

DAIRY FREE
GLUTEN FREE
VEGAN

PREP TIME: 5 MINUTES
COOK TIME: 17 MINUTES

½ peach, chopped
½ nectarine, chopped
½ plum, chopped
1 tablespoon agave nectar
1 teaspoon freshly
    squeezed lemon juice
¼ teaspoon ground
    cinnamon
Pinch salt

1. In a small saucepan over medium-high heat, combine the peach, nectarine, plum, agave nectar, lemon juice, cinnamon, and salt. Cook for about 2 minutes until the compote starts to boil.

2. Reduce the heat to low and stir with a wooden spoon to break up and smash the fruit. Simmer for 10 to 15 minutes, stirring occasionally.

3. This will keep, refrigerated in a jar, for up to 5 days. Or, freeze it in ice cube trays for single-serving cubes ready to heat in the microwave and use.

MAKE IT SEASONAL

Try other flavor combinations like 1 cup of chopped apple, ½ cup of chopped pear, ¼ teaspoon of ground cinnamon, and ⅛ teaspoon of ground nutmeg or allspice. In the summer, try 1 cup of chopped strawberries and 1 cup of fresh blueberries.

Per Serving: Calories: 36; Fat: 0g; Protein: 1g; Carbohydrates: 9g; Fiber: 1g; Sodium: 43mg; Sugar: 4g

Apple Crumble

This delicious apple crumble is a warm treat on a cold morning. You'll feel like you're indulging even though it is made quickly in the microwave. Prepare it in a glass mug and take it to go. The apples and oats are great sources of fiber, and a drizzle of almond butter offers protein and fat. **SERVES 1**

VEGETARIAN

PREP TIME: 5 MINUTES
COOK TIME: 7 MINUTES

For the filling
1 large apple, diced
1½ teaspoons local honey
1 teaspoon freshly
   squeezed lemon juice
½ teaspoon ground
   cinnamon
¼ teaspoon ground nutmeg

For the crumble
1 teaspoon coconut oil
1 teaspoon grass-fed butter
1 tablespoon
   whole-wheat flour
2 tablespoons
   old-fashioned oats
1 tablespoon coconut sugar,
   or granulated sugar
Pinch ground cinnamon
Pinch salt
Vanilla Greek yogurt, for
   topping (optional)
Almond butter, for topping
   (optional)

To make the filling
In a deep microwave-safe bowl or large mug, stir together the apple, honey, lemon juice, cinnamon, and nutmeg. Set aside.

To make the crumble
1. In a small microwave-safe bowl, microwave the coconut oil and butter for 30 seconds until melted.

2. Stir in the flour, oats, coconut sugar, cinnamon, and salt until combined and resembling wet sand. Layer the crumble topping on top of the apple filling.

3. Put the bowl in the microwave and heat for 5 to 6 minutes, or until the apples are bubbly.

4. Let cool for several minutes before eating. Garnish it with vanilla yogurt and a drizzle of almond butter (if using).

Per Serving: Calories: 340; Fat: 10g; Protein: 3g; Carbohydrates: 66g; Fiber: 7g; Sodium: 160mg; Sugar: 44g

Quinoa Porridge, 3 Ways, *Page 41*

CHAPTER 4

Granola, Oats, and Grains

Grains have gotten a bad name with the rise of low-carb and no-carb diets. But, as we discussed earlier, not all carbs are created equal, and our bodies require carbs for a balanced diet. In this section, you will find recipes using healthy, wholesome carbs. You'll learn to make your own granola, spice up your oatmeal routine, and create a few unique porridge-like dishes using less common but very healthy carbs such as quinoa and grits.

Homemade Granola

There is no shortage of granola for sale on the shelves of the grocery store. But it's so easy, and healthier, to make a delicious granola right at home. Start with a few ingredients—oats, oil, and a sweetener such as honey or maple syrup—to make your own version. Once you master the basics, the options for customizing it are endless. Try different nuts and seeds that can bake with the oats and add dried fruit after baking to prevent them from burning. SERVES 6

DAIRY FREE

GLUTEN FREE

VEGETARIAN

PREP TIME: 5 MINUTES

COOK TIME: 20 MINUTES

½ cup coconut oil

½ cup local honey, or pure maple syrup

½ teaspoon ground cinnamon

Pinch salt

3 cups old-fashioned oats

1 cup slivered nuts, such as almonds (optional)

1 cup raisins (optional)

1. Preheat the oven to 300°F. Line a baking sheet with parchment paper or a silicone baking mat.

2. In a large bowl, whisk the coconut oil, honey, cinnamon, and salt until combined. Add the oats and nuts (if using) and stir to coat completely. Spread the mixture onto the prepared baking sheet in a single layer.

3. Bake for 15 to 20 minutes until golden brown, stirring halfway through the baking time.

4. Remove from the oven and stir in the raisins (if using).

5. Let cool and store in airtight container for up to 1 month.

MAKE IT LAST

To maximize shelf life, after cooking, cool the granola completely on the sheet pan before storing in an airtight container.

Per Serving: Calories: 399; Fat: 21g; Protein: 6g; Carbohydrates: 52g; Fiber: 4g; Sodium: 30mg; Sugar: 24g

Grainless Granola

This nutrient-dense mixture of nuts and seeds creates a crunchy snack that will satiate your hunger. Lightly sweetened with honey and dried fruit, this is a great gluten free and grain free, protein-rich breakfast, optimal for someone seeking low-carb dishes. Sprinkle it on top of yogurt or drench it in milk for a tasty breakfast bowl. SERVES 10

DAIRY FREE

GLUTEN FREE

VEGETARIAN

PREP TIME: 10 MINUTES

COOK TIME: 30 MINUTES

3 tablespoons melted
   coconut oil

⅓ cup local honey

2 cups silvered almonds

1½ cups pecans

1 cup cashews

½ cup shredded coconut

3 tablespoons chia seeds

1 tablespoon ground
   flaxseed

2 tablespoons sugar or
   coconut sugar

1 teaspoon ground
   cinnamon

½ teaspoon salt

¼ cup dried fruit (optional)

1. Preheat the oven to 350°F. Line a baking sheet with parchment paper or a silicone baking mat.

2. In a small bowl, stir together the coconut oil and honey.

3. In a medium bowl, stir together the almonds, pecans, cashews, coconut, chia, flaxseed, sugar, cinnamon, and salt until blended. Pour the oil and honey mixture over the nuts and seeds and stir well until evenly coated. Pour the granola mixture onto the prepared baking sheet and press it into a single layer.

4. Bake on the center rack for 20 minutes. Remove and stir. Add the dried fruit (if using) and bake for 5 to 10 minutes more until golden brown.

5. Let cool completely before storing it in an airtight container, where it will keep for several weeks.

Per Serving: Calories: 519; Fat: 44g; Protein: 11g; Carbohydrates: 29g; Fiber: 9g; Sodium: 124mg; Sugar: 15g

Granola Bars

Indulge in the natural sweetness of these homemade granola bars and avoid unwanted preservatives and hidden ingredients found in many store-bought versions. With their dark chocolate chips and a little sea salt, they contain a perfect balance of sweet and salty. MAKES 24 CUBES

VEGETARIAN

PREP TIME: 5 MINUTES
COOK TIME: 7 MINUTES

Nonstick cooking spray

8 tablespoons (1 stick) unsalted grass-fed butter

¼ cup packed light brown sugar

½ cup local honey

1 large egg

2 cups old-fashioned oats

¾ cup whole-wheat flour

½ cup puffed brown rice cereal

½ cup dark chocolate chips

½ teaspoon baking powder

½ teaspoon sea salt

1. Lightly coat an 8-inch microwave-safe baking dish with cooking spray.

2. In a small microwave-safe bowl, soften the butter in the microwave for 15 seconds. Using a fork, whisk in the brown sugar and honey until well combined. Add the egg and stir until combined.

3. In a large bowl, stir together the oats, flour, rice cereal, chocolate chips, baking powder, and salt.

4. Pour in the butter mixture and, using a spatula, stir until all the dry ingredients are well incorporated into the butter mixture. Spread the granola mixture into the prepared baking dish.

5. Microwave for 6 minutes.

6. Let cool. Cut into 24 cubes and store them in an airtight container for up to 1 week.

SMART SHOPPING

Puffed rice cereal is a good gluten free option that is low in calories, but it is best to purchase a brown rice version to get the fiber and other vitamins and minerals without added sugars. Brands like Barbara's, Arrowhead Mills, and Nature's Path make good options.

Per Serving (1 cube): Calories: 115; Fat: 5g; Protein: 2g; Carbohydrates: 17g; Fiber: 1g; Sodium: 43mg; Sugar: 9g

Overnight Oats

Who says oatmeal can only be served hot? Prep this recipe in a jar the night before and enjoy these cool oats on your way out the door. You can make a larger batch to have ready for every morning of the week. Garnish with your favorite toppings to add flavor and variety to your routine. You can also experiment with other milks, such as oat, almond, or soy. **SERVES 1**

GLUTEN FREE
VEGETARIAN

PREP TIME: 5 MINUTES
CHILL TIME: AT LEAST
6 HOURS, OR OVERNIGHT

½ cup old-fashioned oats
½ cup milk
1 tablespoon chia seeds
1 tablespoon pure
   maple syrup
¼ teaspoon vanilla extract
½ cup chopped fruit, such
   as strawberries, bananas,
   peaches, or kiwi
2 tablespoons nuts or
   seeds, such as almonds,
   cashews, pistachios, or
   pumpkin seeds

1. In an 8-ounce mason jar, combine the oats, milk, chia seeds, maple syrup, and vanilla. Stir, cover, and refrigerate overnight.

2. In the morning, top with your choice of fruit and nuts.

THE NIGHT BEFORE
Prepare toppings "packets" for this no-cook recipe in advance to make it easier to grab and go in the morning. Ideas for other flavor combinations: ¼ cup of sliced banana, ¼ cup of sliced strawberries, 2 tablespoons of sliced almonds; or ½ cup of sliced kiwi, 1 tablespoon of shredded coconut, and 1 tablespoon of crushed cashews.

Per Serving: Calories: 392; Fat: 13g; Protein: 13g; Carbohydrates: 59g; Fiber: 11g; Sodium: 65mg; Sugar: 22g

"Zoats" a.k.a. Zucchini Oats

This bowl of delicious, creamy oatmeal is a great way to eat your greens without even realizing it. Shredded zucchini is hard to pinpoint in the dish thanks to the dark chocolate chips and nutty almond butter. SERVES 2

DAIRY FREE

GLUTEN FREE

VEGETARIAN

SUPER-RUSHED

PREP TIME: 2 MINUTES

COOK TIME: 7 MINUTES

2 cups water

1 cup old-fashioned oats

1 cup shredded zucchini

1 large egg

Pinch salt

¼ cup dark chocolate chips

2 tablespoons
   almond butter

1. In a small saucepan over medium-high heat, combine the water, oats, and zucchini. Cook for about 5 minutes until the water is absorbed.

2. Remove the pan from the heat and crack the egg into the saucepan. Stir well and return the pan to low heat. Cook for 2 minutes. Turn off the heat and stir in the salt and chocolate chips.

3. Scoop the mixture into 2 bowls, drizzle each with 1 tablespoon of almond butter, and serve.

MAKE IT CRUNCHY

If you like a little crunch, top the oats with Homemade Granola (page 32) or sliced almonds.

Per Serving: Calories: 359; Fat: 18g; Protein: 13g; Carbohydrates: 42g; Fiber: 6g; Sodium: 117mg; Sugar: 10g

Oatmeal Bowls

Steel cut oats make a thick and creamy oatmeal that is nutty and slightly chewy. Because it is the least processed form of oatmeal, it takes slightly longer to cook. You can let a slow cooker do the work for you or spend a little longer meal prepping for the week to enjoy the benefits of this tasty bowl of oats. **SERVES 2**

GLUTEN FREE

VEGETARIAN

LESS THAN 5 INGREDIENTS

PREP TIME: 2 MINUTES

COOK TIME: 9 HOURS

1 cup steel cut oats

4 cups water

1 tablespoon grass-fed butter

1. In a slow cooker, stir together the oats and water.

2. Cover the cooker and cook on low heat for 8 to 9 hours.

3. In the morning, stir in the butter until melted. Serve with toppings of choice.

COOKING HACK

There are a few ways to alter this recipe so it suits your lifestyle. If you do not have time to prepare steel cut oats, rolled oats are a great option and taste much better than quick-cooking oats. If you don't have a slow cooker, prepare this on the stovetop. In a saucepan over medium heat, combine 1 cup of steel cut oats, 3 cups water, and a pinch of salt. Simmer for 20 minutes, stirring occasionally. Cook for 5 to 10 minutes more, depending on your desired consistency. The steel cut oats will continue to thicken as they cool.

Per Serving: Calories: 391; Fat: 12g; Protein: 14g; Carbohydrates: 58g; Fiber: 10g; Sodium: 15mg; Sugar: 0g

BLT Grits Bowl

Grits are a traditional Southern dish made of ground corn and are naturally gluten free. Quick grits are ground finer and take only 10 minutes to cook versus the typical 30 minutes. To enhance the flavor, cook the grits with milk instead of just water, and season whichever liquid you use with spices that you like. Topping it with bacon, spinach (the "L" in the title is for "leaf," as in spinach leaf!), avocado, and tomato elevates this simple savory dish to a complex flavorful feast. **SERVES 4**

GLUTEN FREE

PREP TIME: 5 MINUTES
COOK TIME: 15 MINUTES

1 cup water
1 cup milk of choice
Pinch salt
1 cup quick cooking grits
2 teaspoons grass-fed butter, divided (optional in the spinach)
1 tablespoon extra-virgin olive oil
½ cup fresh spinach
½ cup grated Parmesan cheese (optional)
½ avocado, sliced
6 cherry tomatoes, halved
2 bacon slices, cooked and chopped
Salt
Freshly ground black pepper

1. In a small saucepan over medium-high heat, combine the water and milk and bring to a boil. Add the salt. Slowly pour in the grits, stirring to prevent them from clumping.

2. Reduce the heat to maintain a simmer and cook for about 7 minutes until the liquid is absorbed, stirring frequently. Remove from the heat and stir in 1 teaspoon of butter.

3. While the grits cook, put a small skillet over medium heat and heat the olive oil.

4. Add the spinach and sauté for 2 minutes to soften. Remove the pan from the heat and stir in the remaining 1 teaspoon of butter (if using) and the Parmesan cheese (if using) until melted and incorporated.

5. Spoon the grits into 4 bowls. Divide the spinach mixture, avocado, tomatoes, and bacon equally among the bowls. Taste and season with salt and pepper, as needed.

6. Refrigerate any leftover grits in an airtight container for up to 5 days. They will thicken and harden as they cool. To make them creamy again, break up the grits and stir in enough boiling water to reach your desired consistency.

Per Serving: Calories: 345; Fat: 17g; Protein: 14g; Carbohydrates: 38g; Fiber: 4g; Sodium: 430mg; Sugar: 4g

Polenta Squares

Polenta is a traditional Italian dish consisting of coarsely ground cornmeal. Typically, it's made by slowly stirring milk and butter into cornmeal while it cooks, creating a creamy dish. This breakfast version doesn't require laboring over the stove. Instead, mix the ingredients and bake them to create a hearty filling casserole. **MAKES 12 SQUARES**

GLUTEN FREE

PREP TIME: 15 MINUTES

COOK TIME: 55 MINUTES

Nonstick cooking spray

4 bacon slices, chopped into 1-inch pieces

½ small onion, diced

½ cup diced mushrooms

½ cup chopped fresh spinach

1 cup chicken broth

1 cup polenta

1 cup milk

2 large eggs

1 teaspoon salt

½ teaspoon garlic powder

¼ teaspoon freshly ground black pepper

1 cup shredded cheese of choice, such as Parmesan, white Cheddar, or smoked Gouda

¼ cup freshly chopped basil (optional)

1. Preheat the oven to 350°F. Lightly coat a 9-by-13-inch baking dish with cooking spray.

2. In a skillet over medium-high heat, cook the bacon for about 5 minutes until cooked through, but not quite crispy. Using a spoon, remove all but 2 tablespoons of fat from the skillet.

3. Return the skillet with the bacon and 2 tablespoons of fat to the stovetop and turn the heat to medium. Add the onion and mushrooms. Sauté for about 3 minutes. Add the spinach. Cook, stirring, for 2 to 3 minutes until wilted. Remove from the heat.

4. In a glass measuring cup, microwave the chicken broth for about 4 minutes until it boils.

5. In a medium bowl, whisk the polenta, milk, eggs, salt, garlic powder, and pepper until combined. Whisk in the spinach and bacon mixture and cheese.

6. While whisking continuously, pour in the hot chicken broth. Immediately pour the polenta mixture into the prepared baking dish.

7. Bake for 15 minutes. Remove from the oven and vigorously stir the polenta. Bake for 25 minutes more.

8. Cut into squares and serve garnished with basil (if using). Leftover polenta squares can be wrapped individually for a grab-and-go option and will keep, refrigerated, for up to 5 days.

Per Serving (1 square): Calories: 145; Fat: 7g; Protein: 8g; Carbohydrates: 12g; Fiber: 1g; Sodium: 384mg; Sugar: 1g

Better than Cereal Muesli

Cereal is one of the most convenient breakfast items but often lacks fiber and can contain high amounts of sugar, making it a less-than-healthy choice. Turn that around by customizing your own. Neither granola nor oatmeal, muesli is a raw blend of nuts, seeds, and oats that, when combined, equals a perfectly crunchy bite. Add in dried fruit for a sweetened, chewy texture. This muesli blend can be made in minutes and stored for a week's worth of breakfast. SERVES 4

DAIRY FREE

GLUTEN FREE

VEGAN

SUPER-RUSHED

PREP TIME: 5 MINUTES

2 cups old-fashioned oats

¼ cup slivered almonds

¼ cup sunflower seeds

½ cup raisins, or other
    dried fruit

1 teaspoon ground
    cinnamon

In a medium bowl, stir together the oats, almonds, sunflower seeds, raisins, and cinnamon until combined. Refrigerate in an airtight container for up to 1 week. It is great topped with cold milk.

MAKE IT YOUR OWN

Mix in these combinations for variety: nuts (cashews, macadamias, pecans pistachios, walnuts), seeds (flax-seed, pepitas, sesame seeds), or dried fruit (blueberries, chopped apricots or figs, cranberries, dates), or coconut flakes.

Per Serving: Calories: 287; Fat: 8g; Protein: 9g; Carbohydrates: 46g; Fiber: 7g; Sodium: 2mg; Sugar: 12g

Quinoa Porridge, 3 Ways

Quinoa is a seed with its origins in South America. It is high in fiber, protein, and B vitamins, making it a great choice for breakfast. Prepare a batch of quinoa using bone broth to amp up the nutritional content (and flavor) and keep it refrigerated. In the morning, measure ½ cup of quinoa into a bowl, add ¼ cup of warmed milk, and top with one of the sweet or savory flavor combinations. The savory porridge is one of my favorites, with its combination of unique textures and flavors. SERVES 6

GLUTEN FREE

PREP TIME: 5 MINUTES
COOK TIME: 20 MINUTES

For the base porridge
1 cup quinoa, rinsed well
1¾ cups chicken bone broth
Pinch salt
¼ cup milk of choice

For the savory porridge
1 tablespoon extra-virgin
    olive oil
1 kale leaf
1 large egg
Salt
Freshly ground
    black pepper

To make the base porridge

1. In a small saucepan over medium-high heat, stir together the quinoa and chicken bone broth and bring to a boil. Reduce the heat to maintain a simmer, cover the pan, and cook for 15 minutes, or until the moisture is absorbed. Turn off the heat and keep covered to let rest for 5 minutes.

2. Sprinkle the salt on top and, using a fork, fluff the quinoa, mixing in the salt. Cool completely and refrigerate in an airtight container until the day of breakfast prep.

3. Heat your milk of choice.

4. Meanwhile, scoop ½ cup of cooked quinoa into a small bowl. Pour the hot milk over the quinoa and stir to combine.

To make the savory porridge

1. In a small skillet over medium heat, heat the olive oil.

2. Add the kale and cook for 1 to 2 minutes. Push the kale to the side of the skillet and add the egg. Fry for 3 minutes and flip. Cook for 2 minutes more. Transfer the kale to the paper towel.

3. Top the base porridge with the kale and egg. Season with salt and pepper.

CONTINUED

For the banana joy porridge

½ banana, sliced

1 tablespoon sliced almonds

1 tablespoon
shredded coconut

1 teaspoon coarsely
chopped dark chocolate

Local honey, for drizzling

Almond butter, for drizzling

**For the seasonal
fruit porridge**

½ peach, sliced

2 tablespoons fresh
blueberries

1 teaspoon chia seeds

Local honey, for drizzling

To make the banana joy porridge

Top the base porridge with the banana, almonds, coconut, and chocolate. Drizzle with the honey and almond butter.

To make the seasonal fruit porridge

Top the base porridge with the peach, blueberries, and chia seeds. Drizzle with the honey.

THE NIGHT BEFORE

Save leftover quinoa from dinner or make a large batch of quinoa on prep day. The recipe here makes enough for 6 breakfast bowls.

Per Serving (base porridge): Calories: 120; Fat: 2g; Protein: 7g; Carbohydrates: 19g; Fiber: 2g; Sodium: 61mg; Sugar: 1g

Per Serving (savory porridge): Calories: 132; Fat: 2g; Protein: 7g; Carbohydrates: 19g; Fiber: 2g; Sodium: 61mg; Sugar: 1g

Per Serving (banana joy porridge): Calories: 298; Fat: 14g; Protein: 11g; Carbohydrates: 44g; Fiber: 5g; Sodium: 100mg; Sugar: 17g

Per Serving (seasonal fruit porridge): Calories: 204; Fat: 4g; Protein: 9g; Carbohydrates: 36g; Fiber: 5g; Sodium: 62mg; Sugar: 16g

Avocado Egg Cups, *Page 58*

CHAPTER 5
Eggs 11 Ways

Eggs are perfectly portioned protein pods that are great for breakfast and can be prepared ahead of time or even when you're super-rushed, making them the ultimate "fast food." How do you like your eggs prepared? Have you tried making them every which way until you've figured out which is best? In this chapter, we will explore numerous ways to prepare an egg—from scrambled to poached to fried to omelets. We will also explore alternate cooking methods, such as using the oven and microwave.

Smoked Salmon Eggs Benedict with "Avo-daise" Sauce

Eggs Benedict has historically been reserved for brunch on a lazy weekend morning, but I'm here to bring it to your daily routine. With a few tweaks, like using the oven to poach an egg, this recipe is easy. And with a few simple ingredient swaps, like smoked salmon as a clean source of protein to replace the typical sodium-filled ham and avocado to replace the butter-rich hollandaise as a source of healthy fat, this dish can be a home run. **SERVES 2**

DAIRY FREE

PREP TIME: 10 MINUTES

COOK TIME: 12 MINUTES

¼ cup water, divided

4 eggs

½ avocado (option to substitute ½ cup plain Greek yogurt)

4 tablespoons extra-virgin olive oil

2 tablespoons freshly squeezed lemon juice

2 tablespoons boiling water (heat 2 minutes in microwave)

½ teaspoon agave nectar

½ teaspoon salt, plus more for seasoning

¼ teaspoon pepper, plus more for seasoning

Pinch of cayenne pepper

2 low-sodium English muffins

¼ cup fresh spinach

8 ounces low-sodium smoked salmon

1. Preheat the oven to 350°F.

2. Pour 1 tablespoon of water into 4 wells of a standard muffin tin.

3. Crack 1 egg into each water-filled well, being careful not to break the yolk.

4. Bake for 12 minutes. The eggs may appear uncooked, and the yolk will still be runny. If you want the eggs less runny, cook them a bit longer.

5. While the eggs are in the oven, in a blender, combine the avocado, olive oil, lemon juice, boiling water, agave nectar, salt, pepper, and cayenne. Blend until well mixed. Taste and season with more salt and pepper, as needed. Set the sauce aside.

6. Arrange 2 muffin halves on each plate. Put a few spinach leaves on the muffins and top each with smoked salmon. Using a slotted spoon, carefully remove the eggs from the muffin tin and top each muffin half with an egg and the "avo-daise" sauce.

COOKING HACK

If you do not have time to make the avo-daise sauce, mash the avocado directly onto the muffin halves.

Per serving: Calories: 744; Fat: 46g; Protein: 38g; Carbohydrates: 38g; Fiber: 4g; Sodium: 1792mg; Sugar: 6g

Eggs in a Basket

The secret to Instagram-worthy fried eggs is using a silicone mold—but that's already been done! This dish is not just picture-perfect, but delicious, too. Skip the mold and have your ingredients do double duty. Use a piece of bread to contain the egg while it cooks and toast your bread at the same time. High in protein, healthy fats, and fiber, this egg dish checks all the nutrition boxes. SERVES 1

VEGETARIAN
SUPER-RUSHED

PREP TIME: 3 MINUTES
COOK TIME: 7 MINUTES

1 slice whole-wheat bread,
  or sourdough bread
2 teaspoons grass-fed
  butter, divided
1 large egg
Salt
Freshly ground
  black pepper
½ avocado, sliced

1. Heat a skillet over medium heat.

2. Use a cup to cut a hole in the center of the bread slice. Save the bread circle so you can use it to soak up the yolk. Spread 1 teaspoon of butter on each side of the bread—don't forget to butter the circle, too. Once the skillet is hot, lay the buttered bread in it and press it down with a spatula. Let cook for about 30 seconds to melt the butter. Flip the bread.

3. Crack the egg into a small ramekin, being careful not to break the yolk. Gently pour the egg into the hole in the bread. Place the buttered circle on the skillet (off to the side). Let cook for about 3 minutes. Using a spatula, gently flip the bread and egg and cook for about 3 minutes more on the other side.

4. When the egg is cooked to your liking, transfer the cooked egg and toast to a plate. Season with salt and pepper. Serve with sliced avocado and the grilled bread round.

SMART SHOPPING
I recommend stocking up on Dave's Killer Bread 21 Whole Grains and Seeds. Ezekiel makes a great sprouted whole-wheat bread, and Oroweat makes a good 100 percent whole-wheat bread.

VARIATION TIP
If you want to make this gluten free, cook the egg in a bell pepper ring.

Per Serving: Calories: 344; Fat: 26g; Protein: 11g; Carbohydrates: 19g; Fiber: 8g; Sodium: 255mg; Sugar: 2g

Easy Egg Muffins

If you are craving eggs and toast for breakfast but just don't have the time to sit down and enjoy a full breakfast spread, these make-ahead egg muffins are a great way to have it all on the go. With a nutrient-dense base and the potential to swap in any chopped veggies you like, this egg dish will let you have your eggs and eat them, too! **MAKES 12 MUFFINS**

PREP TIME: 8 MINUTES

COOK TIME: 12 MINUTES

Olive oil, for preparing the muffin tin

6 slices whole-wheat bread

12 large eggs

¼ cup sour cream, or milk

½ teaspoon salt

¼ teaspoon freshly ground black pepper

¼ cup diced zucchini

¼ cup diced mushrooms

¼ chopped fresh spinach

½ cup shredded cheese of choice

¼ cup cooked bacon (optional)

1. Preheat the oven to 350°F. Lightly coat a standard muffin tin with olive oil.

2. Using a rolling pin, flatten the bread slices. With a cup, cut 2 circles from each flattened bread slice, being careful not to tear the circles; they will become the muffin "liners." Gently press the 12 bread circles into the prepared muffin tin.

3. In a medium bowl, whisk the eggs and sour cream until blended. Season with salt and pepper and whisk to combine. Gently pour the egg mixture into the lined muffin wells.

4. Evenly divide the zucchini, mushrooms, spinach, cheese, and bacon (if using) among the egg-filled wells. If you like, customize each row for different members in the household.

5. Bake for 10 to 12 minutes until set. Remove and let cool before serving.

MAKE IT AHEAD

Make a batch of egg muffins and store them for the week. To store, wrap with a thin layer of parchment paper and cover with plastic wrap to seal. Keep refrigerated for up to 5 days, or freeze for 2 weeks. When it is time to reheat, remove the plastic wrap and heat in the microwave for 30 seconds, if refrigerated, or 1 minute if frozen.

Per Serving (1 muffin): Calories: 128; Fat: 7g; Protein: 9g; Carbohydrates: 7g; Fiber: 1g; Sodium: 237mg; Sugar: 1g

Zucchini Frittata

This recipe is a version of a traditional Italian dish that is filled with fresh vegetables, basil, and eggs. With little sugar or carbs, this vegetarian dish can be served anytime, but it is best served first thing in the morning. Healthy fats and proteins keep you satiated throughout the day and the veggies provide the micronutrients you need to optimize performance. SERVES 6

GLUTEN FREE
VEGETARIAN

PREP TIME: 10 MINUTES
COOK TIME: 25 MINUTES

2 tablespoons extra-virgin olive oil
1 small onion, diced
2 zucchini, sliced
½ teaspoon salt
¼ teaspoon freshly ground black pepper
6 to 8 large eggs
½ cup milk, or sour cream
1 teaspoon dried basil
½ teaspoon garlic salt
¼ cup grated Parmesan cheese

1. Preheat the oven to 375°F.

2. In a large oven-safe skillet over medium heat, heat the olive oil.

3. Add the onion and zucchini and sauté for about 10 minutes until softened. Season with salt and pepper.

4. Meanwhile, in a medium bowl, whisk the eggs and milk until combined. Stir in the basil and garlic salt. Pour the eggs over the cooked veggies. Turn the heat to low and let the eggs set for about 30 seconds. Gently pull the eggs from the edge to the center, letting any uncooked egg fill the space. Cook for 1 to 2 minutes more until the eggs set along the side of the skillet. Sprinkle on the Parmesan cheese.

5. Put the skillet in the oven for about 10 minutes to finish cooking, or until the edges of the frittata are golden brown.

Per Serving: Calories: 161; Fat: 12g; Protein: 10g; Carbohydrates: 4g; Fiber: 1g; Sodium: 336mg; Sugar: 3g

Sous Vide Egg Bites

I've cracked the code on one of the most popular items at your favorite coffee shop, but at a fraction of the price and without the extra stop on the way to work or school. This recipe is perfect for making ahead. These are wonderful to make for family or a group of friends because everyone can create their own combination. If you don't have a sous vide machine, don't fret; these tasty bites can also be made in the microwave. **MAKES 12 BITES**

GLUTEN FREE

PREP TIME: 10 MINUTES
COOK TIME: 1 HOUR
(OR 7 MINUTES IN THE
MICROWAVE)

10 to 12 eggs
½ cup cottage cheese
¼ cup sour cream
1 teaspoon salt
½ teaspoon freshly ground
  black pepper
½ teaspoon garlic powder
2 tablespoons
  grass-fed butter
1 cup shredded cheese
  of choice
½ cup roasted veggies
  (optional)
½ cup sundried tomatoes
  (optional)
½ cup cooked, chopped
  bacon, or sausage
  (optional)

1. Set the sous vide cooker to 172°F, or see cooking hack tip (following).

2. In a food processor or blender, combine the eggs, cottage cheese, sour cream, salt, pepper, and garlic powder. Blend until combined.

3. Coat the inside of 12 (4-ounce) mason jars with the butter.

4. Sprinkle 2 teaspoons of cheese into each jar. Add 2 teaspoons of roasted veggies (if using), 2 teaspoons of sundried tomato (if using), and 2 teaspoons of bacon (if using).

5. Evenly divide the egg mixture among the jars. Sprinkle each with 2 teaspoons of the remaining cheese.

6. Screw on the lids, making sure not to seal them too tightly. Using tongs, slowly lower the jars into the water.

7. Cook for 1 hour. If you plan to store them and reheat later, cook them only for 50 minutes.

8. Let cool. Refrigerate the jars for up to 1 week. To reheat, remove the lids and wrap the jars in paper towel. Microwave for 45 seconds.

COOKING HACK

If you don't have a sous vide machine, lightly coat 5-ounce ramekins or jars with butter (however many will fit into your small baking dish). Layer the bottom with cheese and pour in the egg mixture until half full. Add your toppings of choice. In a microwave-safe container, heat enough water to fill the baking dish, reaching about halfway up the sides of the ramekins, for 2 minutes. Carefully pour the hot water into a small glass baking dish and gently place the ramekins in the hot water. Cover with plastic wrap. Microwave for 3 minutes. Let sit, covered, for 2 minutes before serving.

Per Serving (1 bite): Calories: 137; Fat: 11g; Protein: 9g; Carbohydrates: 1g; Fiber: 0g; Sodium: 368mg; Sugar: 1g

Meal Prep Breakfast Burritos

Preparing a breakfast burrito from scratch can be too tall an order for a workday. Follow this recipe the next time you're craving a breakfast burrito and enjoy them all week or all month. These burritos are fantastic fresh but are just as good after having been frozen and reheated on a hurried workday morning. It's easy to make this recipe vegetarian, if you'd like, and top with avocado, salsa, fresh cilantro, or sour cream to taste. **MAKES 10 BURRITOS**

PREP TIME: 10 MINUTES

COOK TIME: 25 MINUTES

1 pound baby potatoes

3 tablespoons extra-virgin olive oil, divided

3 teaspoons salt, divided

1½ teaspoons freshly ground black pepper, divided

½ teaspoon garlic powder

½ teaspoon paprika

1 pound bacon, cooked (see Perfectly Crisp Bacon, page 67)

12 large eggs

½ cup sour cream

10 (10- to 12-inch) tortillas

1 (15.5-ounce) can low-sodium black beans, drained and rinsed

2 cups shredded cheese, such as Jack, Cheddar, or Colby

1. Preheat the oven to 450°F.

2. Quarter the potatoes and then cut them into pieces as uniform in size as possible so they cook consistently. Put the potatoes on a baking sheet. Add 2 tablespoons of olive oil, 2 teaspoons of salt, 1 teaspoon of pepper, the garlic powder, and paprika. Toss to coat.

3. Roast for 20 to 25 minutes until golden brown and slightly crispy on the edges.

4. While the potatoes roast, prepare the bacon. Line a rimmed sheet pan with foil, making sure to cover all surfaces and secure the foil over the lip of the pan. This will catch the bacon grease. Put a wire rack on top of the prepared sheet pan. Drape the bacon slices over the wire rack, perpendicular to the direction of the wires. It is okay if the bacon touches. Bake for 15 minutes.

5. While the potatoes and bacon cook, prepare the scrambled eggs. In a medium bowl, whisk the eggs and sour cream until well combined.

6. In a large skillet over medium-high heat, heat the remaining 1 tablespoon of olive oil, swirling it to coat the pan.

7. Pour in the eggs and let them settle into a thin layer. Using a spatula, move the outside edge of the eggs inward and let the runny eggs fill the space. Let cook for a few minutes and repeat a few more times until the eggs are cooked. Remove from the heat and season with the remaining 1 teaspoon of salt and ½ teaspoon of pepper.

8. Lay the tortillas on a clean work surface. Sprinkle the cheese over the tortillas to create a barrier between the eggs and tortillas so the burrito does not get soggy.

9. Divide the eggs evenly among the tortillas, placing them in the center. Follow with the potatoes, black beans, and bacon. Fold the tortillas like a burrito. If you are planning to freeze them, let the ingredients cool for 10 minutes before assembling the burritos. Once they have cooled and are assembled, wrap each burrito in foil and then in plastic wrap. Keep frozen for up to 1 month.

THE NIGHT BEFORE

To have an easy breakfast on the go, make a batch of burritos and freeze. In the morning before you start to get ready, preheat the oven to 350°F. Reheat the burritos (in foil) for 10 to 12 minutes. Or remove the foil and microwave for 1 to 2 minutes.

Per Serving (1 burrito): Calories: 556; Fat: 34g; Protein: 26g; Carbohydrates: 37g; Fiber: 5g; Sodium: 1484mg; Sugar: 2g

Sweet Potato Hash

Need some warm Southern comfort on a cold winter morning? Skip the guilty pleasures and enjoy healthy carbs mixed with your favorite dark, leafy greens. This recipe allows for a lot of creativity and customization as it is perfect when paired with a variety of conventional breakfast proteins. You'll start this dish on the stove and finish it in the oven, giving you time to gather the family around the table. This recipe goes great garnished with sliced avocado and serve with toast. SERVES 4

DAIRY FREE
GLUTEN FREE

PREP TIME: 10 MINUTES
COOK TIME: 30 MINUTES

6 ounces bacon, chopped into 1-inch pieces (optional)

1 large sweet potato, cut into ¼-inch cubes

1 cup diced yellow onion (from about ½ onion)

1 red bell pepper, diced

3 cups chopped stemmed kale

Salt

Freshly ground black pepper

4 large eggs

1. Preheat the oven to 400°F.

2. In an oven-safe skillet, like a cast-iron skillet, over medium-high heat, render the bacon (if using), cooking it for 8 to 9 minutes until done but still soft. Using a slotted spoon, transfer the bacon to paper towels and drain some of the fat from the pan, leaving about 2 tablespoons in it.

3. Put the skillet over medium-high heat and add the sweet potatoes, spreading them into an even layer. Cook undisturbed in the bacon fat for about 3 minutes until golden brown.

4. Stir in the onion and red bell pepper. Cook for 3 to 5 minutes until softened.

5. Add the kale and cook for 2 minutes more. Stir in the cooked bacon. Season with salt and pepper. Remove the skillet from the heat.

6. Use the back of a spoon to make 4 wells in the cooked ingredients. Crack 1 egg into each well. Put the skillet in the oven for 10 to 12 minutes until the eggs are set. Cook longer if you prefer your eggs less runny.

Per Serving: Calories: 145; Fat: 5g; Protein: 9g; Carbohydrates: 17g; Fiber: 3g; Sodium: 112mg; Sugar: 5g

A Perfect, Quick, and Easy Omelet

Omelets aren't just for breakfast. Perfect your French-inspired masterpiece in the comfort of your own home with this recipe. Learn a few new techniques to create flawless omelets that are as healthy or indulgent as you like. To save time in the morning, you can sauté veggies and meat, and whisk the eggs the night before while preparing dinner. In the morning, rewhisk the eggs just a tad and start at step three. SERVES 1

GLUTEN FREE

VEGETARIAN

SUPER-RUSHED

PREP TIME: 5 MINUTES

COOK TIME: 5 MINUTES

3 large eggs

1 tablespoon sour cream

¼ teaspoon salt

Pinch freshly ground
   black pepper

Nonstick cooking spray

1 cup spinach, sautéed

1 tablespoon feta cheese

½ cup low-sodium sundried
   tomatoes

1. In a small bowl, vigorously whisk the eggs to whip air into them.

2. Add the sour cream, salt, and pepper. Whisk to combine.

3. It's very important to use the right size pan. For a 3-egg omelet, use a 10-inch or smaller skillet or omelet pan. Heat the pan over medium heat until hot (test that it's hot enough with the back of your hand: Hover your hand, palm up, 2 to 3 inches over the skillet to feel if the pan is ready to cook). Lightly coat the pan with cooking spray.

4. Pour in the eggs and let cook. Do not overwork (touch) the eggs to maintain a fluffy, souffle-like egg omelet.

5. Once the edges turn white, using a spatula, pull one side inward and tip the pan in that direction so the uncooked eggs fill the space. Repeat on the opposite side. Once the eggs are no longer runny on top, turn off the heat.

6. Add the spinach, feta cheese, and sundried toma-toes to one side of the omelet. Using a spatula, flip the unfilled portion on top of the ingredients to form a semicircle.

Per Serving: Calories: 321; Fat: 19g; Protein: 21g; Carbohydrates: 18g; Fiber: 4g; Sodium: 949mg; Sugar: 11g

Leftover Chilaquile Egg Scramble

Went a little overboard on Taco Tuesday? Wednesday morning has you covered. Use the leftovers from last night's dinner to create a delicious breakfast dish using popular dinner proteins and customizing it with your own toppings. Inspired by a traditional Mexican breakfast, this is filled with flavor as you cook and layer on the ingredients. **SERVES 2**

PREP TIME: 5 MINUTES

COOK TIME: 10 MINUTES

2 tablespoons extra-virgin olive oil

4 large low-sodium tortillas, cut into 2- to 3-inch strips

2 cups salsa

2 tablespoons diced green chilies, or jalapeño pepper (optional)

1 (15.5-ounce) can low-sodium black beans, drained and rinsed

Leftover cooked protein, such as shredded chicken, sliced steak, shredded pork

4 large eggs, beaten

Salt

Freshly ground black pepper

1. In a large skillet over medium-high heat, heat the olive oil until it shimmers.

2. Add the tortilla strips to the skillet and brown for about 1 minute per side, 2 to 3 minutes total.

3. Pour in the salsa and add the diced chilies (if using) and stir to combine. Cook for about 1 minute to warm.

4. Add the black beans and protein of choice. Reduce the heat to medium and cook, stirring, for 2 to 3 minutes until heated through. Transfer to a serving plate.

5. In the same skillet, add the beaten eggs and cook until your desired doneness. Pour the eggs over the protein and tortilla mixture. Season with salt and pepper. Serve hot.

MAKE IT TASTIER

Amp up the deliciousness by garnishing with avocado slices, fresh cilantro, and cheese, such as crumbled feta or shredded Jack.

Per Serving: Calories: 637; Fat: 25g; Protein: 39g; Carbohydrates: 70g; Fiber: 18g; Sodium: 898mg; Sugar: 9g

3-Minute Microwave Egg Cups

This recipe is, hands-down, one of my favorites. It is quick, easy, and portable without sacrificing flavor or nutrition; I especially like this dish with Kirkland brand's organic basil pesto. Prep these eggs in a ramekin or 4-ounce microwave-safe bowl, cook in the microwave, and have breakfast ready in under 5 minutes. It may look like a small dish but, thanks to the pesto, it's bursting with flavor. SERVES 1

GLUTEN FREE
SUPER-RUSHED

PREP TIME: 2 MINUTES
COOK TIME: 4 MINUTES

1 slice deli turkey meat
1 large egg
1 tablespoon
   shredded spinach
1 tablespoon pesto (see tip)
1 tablespoon grated
   Parmesan cheese
Salt
Freshly ground
   black pepper

1. Gently lay the turkey slice into the bottom of a ramekin to form a bowl shape.

2. Crack the egg into the ramekin. Top it with the spinach, pesto, and Parmesan cheese.

3. Put the ramekin in the microwave and place a microwave-safe plate on top of it. It is very important not to skip the plate. It prevents the eggs from exploding in the microwave. Heat for 1½ to 2 minutes. Let sit for 2 minutes.

4. Using oven mitts, carefully remove the ramekin from the microwave. Season with salt and pepper.

MAKE IT HOMEMADE
Here's an easy pesto recipe if you want to go the homemade route. In a food processor, combine 3 cups of fresh basil leaves, ¾ cup of extra-virgin olive oil, plus more as needed, ½ cup of walnuts or almonds (or ¼ cup of pine nuts), ½ teaspoon of salt, 3 garlic cloves, peeled, ½ cup of grated Parmesan cheese, and 2 tablespoons of grated Pecorino cheese. Blend until a uniform consistency is achieved, adding more olive oil as needed. Refrigerate in an airtight container for up to 5 days, topped with a drizzle of olive oil to prevent the air from damaging it. It can also be frozen for up to 6 months.

Per Serving: Calories: 223; Fat: 15g; Protein: 19g; Carbohydrates: 3g; Fiber: 0g; Sodium: 232mg; Sugar: 1g

Avocado Egg Cups

Busy mornings barely afford the time to have the "whole nine yards," but this dish is quite the kitchen hack that serves up eggs, bacon, and veggies in about 20 minutes without fussing over the stove. The variety of colors, flavors, and textures seems impossible to achieve in such a short time, but it can be done with this one-pan time saver. Biting into the warm creaminess of the avocado paired with the egg and crisp saltiness of the bacon is the perfect storm of amazing flavors. **SERVES 1**

DAIRY FREE
GLUTEN FREE

PREP TIME: 3 MINUTES
COOK TIME: 18 MINUTES

½ avocado
1 large egg
Pinch salt
Pinch freshly ground
   black pepper
2 bacon slices
2 cherry tomatoes, halved

1. Preheat the oven to 425°F. Line a baking sheet with parchment paper.

2. Using a spoon, gently scoop out a little of the avocado to make room for the egg. Put the avocado in an oven-safe ramekin and place the ramekin on the prepared baking sheet.

3. Crack the egg into the avocado half. Season with salt and pepper.

4. Put the bacon slices and cherry tomato halves, cut-side down, on the baking sheet.

5. Bake for 15 to 18 minutes, or until the whites are no longer runny. Top the egg with the cooked bacon and tomatoes.

COOKING HACK
You may need to remove the bacon and/or tomatoes before the egg has finished cooking because their cook times may differ. Watch them closely.

Per Serving: Calories: 294; Fat: 25g; Protein: 13g; Carbohydrates: 9g; Fiber: 6g; Sodium: 485mg; Sugar: 2g

Breakfast Enchiladas, *Page 72*

CHAPTER 6

Protein Packed

Starting your mornings with protein will help you feel full longer and eat healthier during the day. In fact, studies illustrate that eating more protein in the morning, rather than at later meals, could have overall positive effects on our health. In this chapter, you will find recipes using both traditional animal protein as well as alternative sources such as soy and lentils.

Vegetarian Soy Chorizo Breakfast Tacos

If you've never had soy chorizo, you're in for a treat. It's a bit spicy, extremely flavorful, tastes like chorizo, and packs a protein punch. It's worth a try even if you're not vegan. Use small street taco tortillas to make these breakfast tacos. Garnish with sour cream, salsa, cilantro, and shredded or Cotija cheese for a winning combination. Mission brand sells small flour tortillas called Street Tacos Flour Tortillas, and they are the perfect size. SERVES 4

VEGETARIAN

PREP TIME: 5 MINUTES

COOK TIME: 10 MINUTES

1 tablespoon plus one
   teaspoon extra-virgin
   olive oil, divided
¼ cup diced onion
¼ cup grated sweet potato
6 ounces soy chorizo
½ teaspoon garlic powder
¼ teaspoon salt, plus more
   for seasoning
Pinch freshly ground black
   pepper, plus more for
   seasoning
3 large eggs
¼ cup milk
8 small street taco tortillas,
   or corn tortillas

1. In a medium skillet over medium-high heat, heat 1 teaspoon of olive oil.

2. Add the onion and sauté for 1 minute, until softened.

3. Add the sweet potato, soy chorizo, and garlic powder and season with salt and pepper. Stir to combine. Cook for 5 minutes.

4. Meanwhile, in a small bowl, whisk the eggs, milk, ¼ teaspoon of salt, and pinch of pepper until blended.

5. Add the remaining 1 tablespoon of olive oil to the soy chorizo, then pour the egg mixture into the skillet. Using a spatula, move the eggs around the skillet to scramble and cook for 3 minutes, or to your desired doneness.

6. Place the tortillas on a work surface and fill them with the egg mixture.

SMART SHOPPING

If you don't have soy chorizo but have other crumbled soy meat replacements, use that instead and pan-fry with 2 tablespoons of olive oil, 1 teaspoon of chili powder, 1 teaspoon of ground cumin, 1 teaspoon of salt, ½ teaspoon of paprika, and a dash of cayenne.

Per Serving (2 tacos): Calories: 297; Fat: 16g; Protein: 13g; Carbohydrates: 30g; Fiber: 6g; Sodium: 547mg; Sugar: 4g

Beefed-Up Shakshuka

Shakshuka is a traditional Israeli breakfast dish that contains eggs poached in a homemade tomato sauce of onion, peppers, and garlic. The dish is made with Mediterranean-inspired spices—cumin and paprika—and is best with a little bit of a kick and a slice of sourdough bread for dipping. It is typically a vegetarian dish, but incorporating ground beef or lamb is a great way to "beef up" the protein. **SERVES 2**

DAIRY FREE

GLUTEN FREE

PREP TIME: 10 MINUTES

COOK TIME: 30 MINUTES

3 tablespoons extra-virgin olive oil

½ onion, diced

½ red bell pepper, diced

2 garlic cloves, minced

2 tablespoons tomato paste

1 teaspoon ground cumin

1 teaspoon paprika

½ teaspoon salt, plus more for seasoning

½ teaspoon chili powder

10 ounces ground beef

1 (28-ounce) can diced tomatoes

Freshly ground black pepper

4 large eggs

1. In cast-iron skillet over medium-high heat, heat the olive oil.

2. Add the onion and red bell pepper and sauté for 3 to 4 minutes until the veggies are softened and slightly browned.

3. Stir in the garlic and cook for 1 minute more.

4. Stir in the tomato paste, cumin, paprika, salt, and chili powder. Cook, stirring, until browned and fragrant. Watch closely so it does not burn.

5. Crumble in the ground beef and cook for about 8 minutes until browned and no longer pink.

6. Add the diced tomatoes and stir to combine. Cook for 5 minutes until the liquid evaporates and creates a thick sauce. Season with salt and pepper.

7. With the back of a large spoon, create 4 wells in the mixture. Crack 1 egg into each well. Cook for 10 minutes until the yolks are cooked to your preference.

8. Serve garnished, as desired. I like feta cheese, fresh cilantro, sliced avocado, and a drizzle of olive oil or red chili oil.

Per Serving: Calories: 620; Fat: 41g; Protein: 44g; Carbohydrates: 27g; Fiber: 6g; Sodium: 623mg; Sugar: 15g

Maple Sage Sausage Patties

These sweet and savory breakfast patties are a great choice if you're trying to cut the carbs and load up on protein. Made with ground pork, juicy blueberries, and a light hint of maple syrup, these sausage patties only take 10 minutes to cook in the skillet. Top them with crisped sage and consider serving them alongside a fried egg for a tantalizing breakfast. These will keep in the refrigerator for up to 5 days. Just reheat in the microwave for 1 minute. SERVES 4

DAIRY FREE
GLUTEN FREE

PREP TIME: 10 MINUTES
COOK TIME: 10 MINUTES

1 pound ground pork
1 tablespoon pure
  maple syrup
1 tablespoon chopped fresh
  sage, plus more for garnish
  (optional)
1 teaspoon garlic powder
¾ teaspoon salt
½ teaspoon ground ginger
¼ teaspoon ground allspice
⅛ teaspoon freshly ground
  black pepper
⅓ cup fresh blueberries
1 tablespoon extra-virgin
  olive oil

1. In a medium bowl, mix together the ground pork, maple syrup, sage, garlic powder, salt, ginger, allspice, and pepper until well combined.

2. Gently stir in the blueberries. Form the mixture into 8 equal patties and set aside.

3. In a large cast-iron or heavy-bottomed skillet over medium-high heat, heat the olive oil.

4. Add the patties to the skillet and cook for 3 to 4 minutes per side. While cooking the patties, crisp a few fresh sage leaves in the same skillet to use as garnish (if using).

MAKE IT HEALTHIER
To reduce the fat content in this recipe, use ground turkey or chicken instead of pork.

Per Serving (2 patties): Calories: 285; Fat: 20g; Protein: 20g; Carbohydrates: 6g; Fiber: 1g; Sodium: 419mg; Sugar: 4g

Brussels Sprouts and Crispy Bacon One-Pan Hash

This is not your mama's boiled Brussels sprouts. If you're Brussels sprouts–averse, this recipe might change your mind. Brussels sprouts and bacon are a match made in heaven. The salty, crisp bacon partners with the nutty, savory sprout. This one-pan hash can be prepped ahead and makes your morning easy. **SERVES 6**

DAIRY FREE

GLUTEN FREE

PREP TIME: 10 MINUTES

COOK TIME: 20 MINUTES

1 pound Brussels sprouts, trimmed, halved, or quartered if large

1 pound petite potatoes, such as red, baby Yukon gold, or fingerling, diced

8 ounces bacon, or turkey bacon, chopped into 1-inch pieces

1 tablespoon extra-virgin olive oil

1 teaspoon salt

½ teaspoon freshly ground black pepper

1. Preheat the oven to 425°F. Line a baking sheet with parchment paper or a silicone baking mat.

2. On the prepared baking sheet, combine the Brussels sprouts, potatoes, bacon, olive oil, salt, and pepper. Toss to coat the ingredients evenly and spread into a single layer.

3. Bake for 20 minutes, or until the potatoes are soft and starting to turn slightly golden.

MAKE IT HEARTIER

Substitute sweet potatoes for the petite potatoes to increase fiber content. If you would like to add eggs to the dish, remove the baking sheet from the oven after 10 minutes and create 4 wells in the mixture. Crack 1 egg into each well and bake for 10 minutes more, or until the eggs are done to your liking.

Per Serving: Calories: 310; Fat: 19g; Protein: 17g; Carbohydrates: 19g; Fiber: 5g; Sodium: 985mg; Sugar: 3g

Lox Wrap

Think traditional lox bagel meets wrap. This breakfast won't weigh you down. It is light, refreshing, and offers a no-cook recipe for the busiest of mornings. This wrap takes only minutes to make and is filled with omega-3 fatty acids, thanks to the smoked salmon. Paired with crispy veggies, it's just the brain food you need. SERVES 1

SUPER-RUSHED

PREP TIME: 5 MINUTES

1 tortilla

1 teaspoon cream cheese, at
   room temperature

1 tomato slice, halved

½ Persian cucumber, sliced

1 ounce smoked salmon

½ teaspoon capers

Salt

Freshly ground
   black pepper

1 teaspoon fresh dill
   (optional)

1. Lay the tortilla on a work surface and spread the cream cheese onto it.

2. In the center of the tortilla, put the tomato, cucumber, salmon, capers, and dill (if using) and season with salt and pepper. Wrap up the tortillas like a burrito and eat cold.

Per Serving: Calories: 109; Fat: 3g; Protein: 7g; Carbohydrates: 14g; Fiber: 3g; Sodium: 531mg; Sugar: 1g

Perfectly Crisp Bacon

There are several methods to make bacon, but none is easier (and cleaner) than this oven method. Using a wire rack allows the grease to drip off the bacon and create a perfectly crisp, Pinterest-worthy slice without the grease splatter and hassle. Put it in the oven and forget it (for 20 minutes) while you go about other morning or meal prep activities. **SERVES 6**

DAIRY FREE

GLUTEN FREE

LESS THAN 5 INGREDIENTS

PREP TIME: 2 MINUTES

COOK TIME: 20 MINUTES

1 pound bacon, sliced

1. Preheat the oven to 400°F. Line a rimmed sheet pan with foil, making sure to cover all surfaces and secure the foil over the lip of the pan. This will catch the bacon grease. Put a wire rack on top of the prepared sheet pan. Drape the bacon slices over the wire rack, perpendicular to the direction of the wires. It is okay if the bacon slices touch.

2. Bake for 20 minutes, or until perfectly crispy.

MAKE IT SWEET

To make a sweeter bacon variation, in a small bowl, stir together ½ cup of packed light brown sugar and ½ teaspoon of freshly ground black pepper until mixed. Coat the bacon on both sides with the mixture and cook as instructed. This pairs well with the Sweet Potato Breakfast Biscuits (page 108).

SMART SHOPPING

Be particular when buying bacon. It is best to buy bacon that is low sodium, nitrate free, and sugar free. Applegate and Nature's Rancher make good selections. Of course, turkey bacon, and better yet, Canadian bacon, are healthy alternatives, too.

Per Serving: Calories: 161; Fat: 12g; Protein: 12g; Carbohydrates: 1g; Fiber: 0g; Sodium: 431mg; Sugar: 0g

Pancake-Battered Breakfast Sausage Corn Dogs

This recipe is a healthier take on pancakes with a side of sausage because it uses coconut oil, whole wheat flour, and a touch of real maple syrup. Prep these corn dogs ahead using store-bought sausage links. Fry a batch on a weekend, freeze them individually, and reheat in the morning to have a yummy breakfast on the go. **SERVES 12**

PREP TIME: 10 MINUTES

COOK TIME: 15 MINUTES

20 ounces coconut oil

12 turkey sausage links
   (I like Applegate brand)

1¼ cups whole-wheat flour

½ cup cornmeal

1½ teaspoons
   baking powder

½ teaspoon ground
   cinnamon

¼ teaspoon salt

½ cup whole milk

1 large egg

2 tablespoons pure
   maple syrup, plus more
   for dipping

1. Line a plate with paper towels and set aside.

2. In a Dutch oven or heavy-bottomed pot over medium-high heat, heat the coconut oil until the temperature reaches 360°F. Adjust the heat to about medium to maintain the oil's temperature.

3. While the coconut oil heats, prepare the sausage according to the package directions and transfer to the prepared plate to drain and cool. Insert a candy apple stick (or ice pop stick) into the bottom of each sausage.

4. In a medium bowl, whisk the flour, cornmeal, baking powder, cinnamon, and salt until combined. Stir in the milk, egg, and maple syrup until a smooth batter forms.

5. One at a time, dip each sausage into the batter to coat it evenly. Repeat with 2 more sausages.

6. Working in batches so as not to crowd the pot, hold a battered sausage by the stick and gently submerge the tip of the battered sausage in the hot oil for about 5 seconds. Carefully let the sausage slip (with the stick) into the oil. Repeat with 2 more battered sausages. Cook for 2 minutes, flip, and cook for 2 minutes more. Using tongs, transfer the cooked sausages to the prepared plate and repeat with the remaining sausages.

7. Serve immediately with maple syrup on the side, or cool, wrap in foil, and freeze for up to 1 month to reheat later. Reheat in the oven at 350°F for 12 minutes without thawing, or in the microwave for 1 minute.

COOKING HACK

You can use vegetable oil as a coconut oil alternative. If you do not want to fry the corn dogs, use a mini muffin tin and fill the wells three-quarters full with batter. Slice the cooked sausage links into thirds, if using mini sausages, or quarters if regular size. Press a sausage piece into the batter and bake in a 375°F oven for 8 to 10 minutes until the batter is set and cooked through.

Per Serving: Calories: 234; Fat: 13g; Protein: 11g; Carbohydrates: 20g; Fiber: 1g; Sodium: 241mg; Sugar: 4g

Zucchini and Sausage Casserole

Casseroles are the original one-pan dish that gained popularity in the 1950s. Every casserole has three main components: a protein, a filler, and a binder. This recipe calls for ground sausage as the protein, zucchini in place of a traditional filler like potatoes, and egg as the binder. Topped with shredded cheese, this casserole makes a hearty breakfast and a delicious way to start the day. It's also great to customize with different proteins and veggies. **SERVES 12**

PREP TIME: 15 MINUTES

COOK TIME: 1 HOUR

1 pound ground sausage

3 cups cubed zucchini (about 1½ pounds)

1 (4.5-ounce) can diced green chilies

4 large eggs

½ cup milk

2 cups shredded Jack cheese, divided

3 tablespoons all-purpose flour, or white whole-wheat flour

2 tablespoons dried parsley

½ teaspoon salt

1. Preheat the oven to 350°F.

2. In a skillet over medium-high heat, cook the ground sausage for about 8 minutes, crumbling it with a spoon, until no longer pink.

3. Add the zucchini and cook for 8 minutes more, until soft.

4. Meanwhile, in a medium bowl, whisk the green chilies, eggs, milk, 1 cup of Jack cheese, flour, parsley, and salt until combined.

5. Spread the cooked sausage and zucchini into a 9-by-13-inch casserole dish. Cover with the egg mixture. Sprinkle the remaining 1 cup of cheese on top.

6. Bake for 30 to 45 minutes, or until a toothpick inserted into the center of the casserole comes out clean.

THE NIGHT BEFORE

Assemble this casserole at night and refrigerate it uncooked. The next morning, preheat the oven and bake the casserole. You can refrigerate leftovers, covered, for up to 5 days. To make grab-and-go portions ahead, let the casserole cool completely then cut it into squares. Refrigerate in an airtight container for up to 5 days.

Per Serving: Calories: 231; Fat: 17g; Protein: 14g; Carbohydrates: 6g; Fiber: 1g; Sodium: 475mg; Sugar: 2g

Curried Lentil Breakfast Bowl

This is a non-typical breakfast dish that is not only nutritious but also quite delicious. Lentils are an excellent source of protein and fiber, making them a great choice for breakfast. This dish is inspired by Indian curries, which are known for their flavor. It is so good, you will want to lick the bowl clean. SERVES 2

DAIRY FREE
GLUTEN FREE

PREP TIME: 8 MINUTES
COOK TIME: 12 MINUTES

1 tablespoon plus
   1 teaspoon extra-virgin
   olive oil, divided
1 garlic clove, minced
¼ onion, diced
2 chicken sausage
   links, sliced
⅓ cup tomato sauce
1 teaspoon curry powder
½ teaspoon ground cumin
½ teaspoon salt, plus more
   for seasoning
¼ teaspoon smoked paprika
⅛ teaspoon freshly ground
   pepper, plus more for
   seasoning
2 cups cooked lentils
2 cups fresh spinach
2 fried eggs

1. In a large skillet over medium-high heat, heat 1 tablespoon of olive oil.

2. Add the garlic, onion, and sausage pieces. Sauté for 3 to 5 minutes until the onion is translucent.

3. Using a wooden spoon, stir in the tomato sauce, curry powder, cumin, salt, paprika, and pepper, scraping up any browned bits on the bottom and sides of the skillet to deglaze the pan.

4. Stir in the cooked lentils. Cook for about 3 minutes, or until the lentils are heated through. Scoop the lentil mixture into two bowls.

5. Return the skillet to the heat, add the remaining 1 teaspoon olive oil and the spinach, and sauté for about 2 minutes until the spinach wilts. Divide the spinach between the lentil bowls. Top each with a fried egg and season with salt and pepper.

Per Serving: Calories: 487; Fat: 20g; Protein: 31g; Carbohydrates: 49g; Fiber: 18g; Sodium: 855mg; Sugar: 7g

Breakfast Enchiladas

Use a rotisserie chicken or dinner leftovers to create a delicious breakfast. These enchiladas are creamy and chewy thanks to sour cream, cheese, and shredded chicken. Whip up a batch for the week and reheat single servings in the microwave in the morning. Garnish with sour cream, sliced avocado, and salsa as desired. **SERVES 6**

PREP TIME: 7 MINUTES

COOK TIME: 40 MINUTES

1¼ cups shredded, cooked chicken

¼ cup minced onion

¼ cup canned diced green chilies

¼ cup plus 1 tablespoon sour cream

1 cup shredded cheese of choice, divided

1 teaspoon garlic salt

½ teaspoon salt

6 tortillas

6 large eggs

½ cup milk

1. Preheat the oven to 375°F.

2. In a small bowl, stir together the chicken, onion, green chilies, sour cream, ½ cup of shredded cheese, garlic salt, and salt.

3. Place the tortillas on a work surface and fill each with the chicken mixture. Roll the tortillas and place them seam-side down in a baking dish, nestling each next to the other to pack them in tightly.

4. In a medium bowl, whisk the eggs and milk until blended. Pour the egg mixture over the tortillas and use a spatula to press each roll in place. Sprinkle the remaining ½ cup of cheese on top. Cover the dish with foil.

5. Bake for 30 minutes. Remove the foil and bake for 5 to 10 minutes more.

THE NIGHT BEFORE

If making the night before, pour the egg and milk mixture over the enchiladas and let it soak overnight, covered, in the refrigerator. This will help make the dish nice and fluffy. In the morning, put it directly into the oven, covered with foil.

Per Serving: Calories: 274; Fat: 15g; Protein: 21g; Carbohydrates: 14g; Fiber: 2g; Sodium: 357mg; Sugar: 2g

Bacon, Brie, and Apple Sandwich, *Page 83*

CHAPTER 7

Sandwiches and Toast

Who could have predicted the recent toast phenomenon? Restaurants and cafés are serving up toasted bread topped with unique flavor combinations because toast's popularity has reached an all-time high. This chapter shares how to make your own restaurant-quality avocado toast and sandwiches, along with healthier alternatives for bagel toppings, and ways to incorporate sweet potatoes into your toast habit.

Elevated Avocado Toast

Avocado toast is everywhere and rightfully so. It is the perfect breakfast—complete with fiber, healthy fats, and lots of flavor. Buttery avocado on crispy toast is taken to the next level when topped with essential vitamins and minerals thanks to the small but mighty sprinkle of microgreens and cherry tomatoes. SERVES 1

VEGETARIAN
SUPER-RUSHED

PREP TIME: 7 MINUTES
COOK TIME: 3 MINUTES

2 slices bread

2 tablespoons pesto

1 avocado, halved

4 cherry tomatoes,
   cut into slices

1 tablespoon grated
   Parmesan cheese

1 tablespoon microgreens

Salt

Freshly ground
   black pepper

1. Toast the bread. If you're in a hurry, use the toaster; if you have more time, grill the bread in a cast iron skillet on the stovetop until golden, about 3 minutes.

2. Spread 1 tablespoon of pesto on each piece of toast.

3. Using a spoon, gently scoop the avocado onto the bread (½ avocado per slice). Use a fork to mash the avocado onto the bread.

4. Press the tomatoes into the avocado. Sprinkle Parmesan cheese and microgreens on top and season with salt and pepper.

Per Serving: Calories: 522; Fat: 30g; Protein: 14g; Carbohydrates: 53g; Fiber: 22g; Sodium: 432mg; Sugar: 5g

Savory Smoked Salmon Sweet Potato Bagel

Ditch the processed carbs from traditional bagels and make your own sweet potato "bagel" packed with fiber. Amp it up with protein from smoked salmon and substitute a smashed avocado for the cream cheese layer. Slice and bake a batch of sweet potatoes to have them ready to toast during busy mornings. SERVES 4

DAIRY FREE

GLUTEN FREE

PREP TIME: 10 MINUTES

COOK TIME: 25 MINUTES

For the bagel seasoning

2 tablespoons poppy seeds

1 tablespoon white
  sesame seeds

1 tablespoon black
  sesame seeds

1 tablespoon dried
  minced garlic

1 tablespoon dried
  minced onion

2 teaspoons salt

For the bagel

1 large sweet potato,
  cut lengthwise into
  ¼-inch-thick slices

1 tablespoon extra-virgin
  olive oil

1 avocado, smashed

4 ounces sliced low-sodium
  smoked salmon

¼ red onion, thinly sliced

¼ cup cherry tomatoes, cut
  into slices

To make the bagel seasoning

In a small bowl, stir together the poppy seeds, white and black sesame seeds, garlic, onion, and salt. Set aside.

To make the bagel

1. Preheat the oven to 350°F.

2. Place the sweet potato slices in a single layer on a baking sheet. Brush with the olive oil.

3. Bake for 20 minutes, or until softened. At this point, once cooled, they can be refrigerated in an airtight container for up to 1 week to be used later.

4. To continue with the recipe, toast the baked sweet potato slices in a toaster oven until browned.

5. Spread the smashed avocado over the sweet potato slices and add a few pieces of smoked salmon to each.

6. Layer the red onion and tomatoes on top and sprinkle the bagel seasoning on top.

BAKE AHEAD

The bagel seasoning recipe makes about a half cup. Store it in an airtight container at room temperature, and sprinkle it on your favorite breakfast dishes, such as hard-boiled eggs, toast, or baked potatoes.

Per Serving: Calories: 208; Fat: 15g; Protein: 8g; Carbohydrates: 14g; Fiber: 5g; Sodium: 457mg; Sugar: 3g

Sweet Potato Toast

Did you know that yams sold in the United States are actually sweet potatoes and that there are several varieties that range in color from white, to purple, to orange? This tuber-meets-toast recipe is a great option if you are cutting out processed breads or gluten. Sweet potatoes are high in fiber and very versatile to cook with. Top the "toast" with your favorite nut butter and banana and play around with different combinations. SERVES 1

DAIRY FREE

GLUTEN FREE

PREP TIME: 10 MINUTES

COOK TIME: 25 MINUTES

1 large sweet potato,
   cut lengthwise into
   ¼-inch-thick slices

1 tablespoon almond butter

1 banana, sliced

1 tablespoon chia seeds

1 tablespoon crumbled
   cooked bacon

1. Preheat the oven to 350°F.

2. Place the sweet potato slices in a single layer on a baking sheet.

3. Bake for 20 minutes, or until softened.

4. To prepare one serving of toast, toast 2 slices of sweet potato in a toaster oven or toaster, until browned.

5. Spread almond butter on each slice.

6. Add the banana slices and sprinkle the chia seeds and bacon on top.

THE NIGHT BEFORE

When prepping meals in advance, slice the sweet potatoes and bake in the oven. You can refrigerate them in an airtight container for up to 1 week and simply pull out what you need each morning and toast just as you would bread.

Per Serving: Calories: 409; Fat: 16g; Protein: 11g; Carbohydrates: 62g; Fiber: 13g; Sodium: 186mg; Sugar: 21g

Make-Ahead Bacon, Egg, and Cheese Breakfast Sandwich

The bacon, egg, and cheese sandwich is possibly the most popular breakfast in the United States because of its delicious combination of flavors. This recipe is a guideline for making a bulk batch in advance to fuel your busy mornings. You will prepare eggs in the oven and customize and fill the eggs with diced veggies. After baking, cut them into circles and assemble your sandwiches. You can easily switch out the bacon for sausage or experiment with various flavor combinations (such as diced green chilies, jalapeños, and Jack cheese, or diced bell pepper, diced mushroom, and sautéed spinach). **MAKES 6 SANDWICHES**

PREP TIME: 10 MINUTES

COOK TIME: 10 MINUTES

Nonstick cooking spray

6 large eggs

½ cup milk

¼ teaspoon salt

⅛ teaspoon freshly ground
   black pepper

6 English muffins, split
   and toasted

½ cup diced veggies of
   choice (optional)

12 bacon slices, cooked (see
   Perfectly Crisp Bacon,
   page 67)

6 slices cheese of choice,
   such as Cheddar, Gouda,
   or Swiss

1. Preheat the oven to 350°F. Coat a small, shallow baking dish with cooking spray.

2. In a medium bowl, whisk the eggs and milk until blended and pour into the prepared baking dish.

3. Bake for 10 minutes, or until the eggs are thoroughly cooked and set. Check for doneness by gently shaking the dish back and forth to make sure the center is cooked through. Remove and season with salt and pepper. Let cool.

4. Using a small paring knife, trace an English muffin outline onto the eggs and cut out 6 circles from the baked egg.

5. Put the English muffins halves on a work surface, cut-side up. Put an egg round on each muffin bottom. Layer the veggies (if using), 2 slices of bacon, and a slice of cheese. Close the sandwiches with the top halves. If storing for later, let cool completely. Wrap each sandwich in parchment paper, then plastic wrap. Refrigerate for up to 5 days, or freeze for up to 2 weeks. To reheat later, remove the wrapping and microwave for 30 seconds to 1 minute.

Per Serving (1 sandwich): Calories: 422; Fat: 23g; Protein: 25g; Carbohydrates: 28g; Fiber: 2g; Sodium: 521mg; Sugar: 4g

Breakfast Bruschetta, 2 Ways

Bruschetta originated in Italy and is, typically, toasted bread soaked in olive oil with fresh tomatoes, garlic, and basil on top. For this breakfast, we are switching it up to make a sweet dish. Topped with a blend of cottage cheese and honey, layered with sliced fresh fruit, and getting the crunch from nuts and seeds, this is a wonderful breakfast to enjoy the fruits of summer. **SERVES 1**

VEGETARIAN

SUPER-RUSHED

PREP TIME: 10 MINUTES

For the base

2 slices Italian bread

2 teaspoons extra-virgin olive oil

¼ cup cottage cheese

1 teaspoon local honey

For the berry almond basil option

1 strawberry, hulled and sliced

1 tablespoon fresh blueberries

1 teaspoon sliced almonds

2 fresh basil leaves, cut into chiffonade

For the peach blueberry mint option

¼ peach, sliced

1 tablespoon fresh blueberries

2 fresh mint leaves, chopped

½ teaspoon chia seeds

To make the base

1. Preheat the broiler and put an oven rack 6 inches from the heat.

2. Brush the bread with the olive oil and put it on a baking sheet. Broil for 2 to 4 minutes until golden brown. You can also do this in a toaster oven for quicker results.

3. In a small bowl, stir together the cottage cheese and honey until well blended. Spread the cottage cheese mixture on the toast.

To make the berry almond basil option

After making the base, layer the strawberry slices, blueberries, almonds, and basil on top.

To make the peach blueberry mint option

After making the base, layer the peach slices, blueberries, mint, and chia seeds on top.

SMART SHOPPING

Purchase seasonal produce to enjoy a variety of fruits year-round.

Per Serving (base): Calories: 245; Fat: 11g; Protein: 12g; Carbohydrates: 26g; Fiber: 1g; Sodium: 438mg; Sugar: 7g

Per Serving (berry almond basil): Calories: 266; Fat: 11g; Protein: 12g; Carbohydrates: 29g; Fiber: 2g; Sodium: 438mg; Sugar: 9g

Per Serving (peach blueberry mint): Calories: 275; Fat: 11g; Protein: 14g; Carbohydrates: 31g; Fiber: 2g; Sodium: 438mg; Sugar: 11g

Crudités Bagel

Bagels are typically high in calories and don't provide many nutrients. They can be a healthy breakfast choice, however, if you opt for whole wheat with healthy toppings. Use avocado for a creamy base layer and arrange a rainbow of crisp vegetables on top for a beautiful presentation that will make your taste buds sing. SERVES 1

VEGETARIAN

SUPER-RUSHED

PREP TIME: 10 MINUTES

1 avocado, halved

1 whole-wheat bagel, toasted or untoasted

1 small Persian cucumber, sliced

1 tomato, sliced

1 radish, sliced

Microgreens, for garnish

1 tablespoon crumbled goat cheese

Salt

Freshly ground black pepper

Bagel Seasoning (page 77), for garnish

1 tablespoon toasted sunflower seeds (optional)

1. Using a fork, spread half the avocado over each bagel half, mashing it to your desired consistency.

2. Layer the cucumber, tomato, radish, and micro-greens on top. Press the goat cheese on top. Season with salt, pepper, and bagel seasoning and top with sunflower seeds (if using).

Per Serving: Calories: 608; Fat: 31g; Protein: 19g; Carbohydrates: 67g; Fiber: 22g; Sodium: 309mg; Sugar: 14g

Caprese Sandwich

Caprese is an Italian salad combining tomato and fresh buffalo mozzarella cheese garnished with fresh basil, a drizzle of olive oil, and a sprinkle of salt and pepper. Put these popular ingredients between 2 slices of toast to create an unexpectedly flavorful and fresh breakfast. SERVES 1

VEGETARIAN

SUPER-RUSHED

PREP TIME: 5 MINUTES

COOK TIME: 10 MINUTES

2 slices Italian bread, or
   French bread

1 tablespoon grass-fed
   butter (optional)

4 slices fresh
   mozzarella cheese

4 slices tomato

Salt

Freshly ground
   black pepper

2 tablespoons pesto (see
   3-Minute Microwave
   Egg Cups for an easy
   homemade recipe or store
   recommendation, page 57)

1 tablespoon grated
   Parmesan cheese

1. Toast the bread. If you are in a hurry, toast it in the toaster; if you have time, preheat the oven to 350°F.

2. Spread the butter on the bread and put it on a baking sheet. Toast in the oven for 10 minutes, or until browned.

3. On one piece of toast, layer 2 mozzarella slices and 2 tomato slices. Repeat.

4. Season with salt and pepper. Drizzle on the pesto and sprinkle Parmesan cheese on top. Close the sandwich with the remaining piece of toast.

Per Serving: Calories: 726; Fat: 52g; Protein: 29g; Carbohydrates: 34g; Fiber: 2g; Sodium: 550mg; Sugar: 3g

Bacon, Brie, and Apple Sandwich

This heavenly sandwich is a combination of sweet and savory, with a mix of crispy apple, creamy Brie, and salty bacon. Add a little arugula for a slightly bitter bite. This recipe works well with pears, too. **SERVES 1**

PREP TIME: 5 MINUTES

COOK TIME: 10 MINUTES

2 slices bread of choice

1 teaspoon grass-fed butter, or extra-virgin olive oil

2 ounces Brie cheese

½ apple, thinly sliced

4 bacon slices, cooked

¼ cup arugula

1. Preheat the oven to 400° F.

2. Brush the bread with butter.

3. Spread half the Brie on each bread slice and put the bread on a baking sheet.

4. Bake for 10 minutes, until the Brie softens and the bread crisps.

5. When the bread is crisp, layer the apple slices, bacon, and arugula. Close the sandwich and halve to serve. It is best eaten warm.

Per Serving: Calories: 573; Fat: 34g; Protein: 26g; Carbohydrates: 42g; Fiber: 4g; Sodium: 649mg; Sugar: 14g

Tofu "Egg" Salad Sandwich

Tofu originated in China around 2,000 years ago. It is made of soybean curds, is a great source of iron and calcium, and is naturally gluten free and low in calories. Overall, this is a great source of protein, especially for anyone who doesn't eat animal protein. This recipe turns tofu into a delicious "egg" salad. SERVES 4

DAIRY FREE
VEGETARIAN
SUPER-RUSHED

PREP TIME: 10 MINUTES

8 slices bread of choice

8 ounces firm tofu

1 tablespoon mayonnaise, or vegan mayonnaise

1 teaspoon freshly squeezed lemon juice

½ teaspoon mustard

¼ teaspoon salt, plus more for seasoning

⅛ teaspoon freshly ground black pepper, plus more for seasoning

Pinch paprika

1 tomato, cut into slices

1. If you are preparing the sandwiches to eat now, toast the bread.

2. In a medium bowl, using the back of a fork, smash the tofu into crumbles.

3. Stir in the mayonnaise, lemon juice, mustard, salt, pepper, and paprika until the mixture resembles egg salad.

4. Season the tomato slices with salt and pepper.

5. Scoop the "egg" salad onto the toast and top with tomato and a second slice of toast.

LOVE YOUR LEFTOVERS

Make a batch of this salad for the week ahead. It can be refrigerated in an airtight container and used in sandwiches or salads as needed.

Per Serving: Calories: 196; Fat: 6g; Protein: 12g; Carbohydrates: 26g; Fiber: 5g; Sodium: 341mg; Sugar: 4g

Krispy Kale Sandwich

Fried eggs are quick and easy to make and good for topping your favorite toast or sandwich. This recipe is great when the yolk oozes onto the crispy kale. This is a vegetarian option; if you like meat, add a slice of bacon. **SERVES 2**

VEGETARIAN

PREP TIME: 3 MINUTES

COOK TIME: 10 MINUTES

4 slices bread, such as whole wheat or French

1 tablespoon extra-virgin olive oil

2 cups torn, stemmed kale

½ teaspoon garlic salt

2 large eggs

½ tomato, sliced

Pinch salt

2 tablespoons shaved Parmesan cheese

1. Toast the bread.

2. In a large cast-iron skillet over medium-high heat, heat the olive oil.

3. Place the kale in the skillet on one side to begin crisping. Let cook on one side for about 3 minutes, flip, and season with garlic salt.

4. Crack the eggs into skillet on the other side. For over-easy eggs, cook for 3 minutes so the egg whites set before flipping. Flip and cook for 1 minute more; for over-medium eggs cook for 3 minutes, flip, and cook for 2 to 3 minutes more; for over-hard eggs, cook for 4 to 5 minutes after flipping so the yolk is completely set.

5. Season the tomato with salt.

6. Assemble the sandwich: Top 1 piece of toast with half the tomato, 1 egg, half the crisped kale, 1 tablespoon of Parmesan cheese, and a second piece of toast. Repeat for a second sandwich.

LOVE YOUR LEFTOVERS

To make a big batch of baked kale, preheat the oven to 275°F. Line a baking sheet with parchment paper. Using 1 head of kale, remove the leaves from each stem, put them in a bowl, drizzle with 2 tablespoons of olive oil, and sprinkle with salt and pepper. Squeeze in some fresh lemon juice and gently massage the kale to break down the fibers. Put the kale on the prepared baking sheet. Bake for 20 to 25 minutes, until the leaves' edges turn slightly brown. Check frequently toward the end of the baking time so the leaves don't burn.

Per Serving: Calories: 305; Fat: 14g; Protein: 16g; Carbohydrates: 32g; Fiber: 5g; Sodium: 421mg; Sugar: 16g

French Toast Roll-Ups, *Page 89*

CHAPTER 8

Pancakes, Waffles, and French Toast

Although traditional pancakes, waffles, and French toast tend to be less nutrient dense, by making a few simple swaps they can still have a place in your breakfast routine, even when you're trying to eat healthy. All you have to do is increase the fiber and protein in these dishes and change the toppings. In this chapter, you will find pancakes, savory waffles, crêpes, and some fun spins on French toast, all with a healthy twist.

French Toast Muffins

Pain perdu translates to "lost bread." If you have a loaf of French bread that is slightly stale or "lost," soak it in milk and egg to bring it back to life. These muffins are a mix of bread pudding and traditional French toast. You will use a muffin tin to bake this recipe and create mini breakfast treats. **MAKES 12 MUFFINS**

VEGETARIAN

PREP TIME: 10 MINUTES

COOK TIME: 20 MINUTES

Nonstick cooking spray

4 large eggs

1½ cups milk

2 tablespoons pure
   maple syrup, plus more
   for serving

2 teaspoons vanilla extract

1 teaspoon ground
   cinnamon

¼ teaspoon ground nutmeg

⅛ teaspoon salt

10 slices bread of choice,
   such as French, Italian,
   or whole wheat, cut into
   ½-inch cubes

½ cup fresh blueberries
   (optional)

Pinch sugar

1. Preheat the oven to 375°F. Generously coat a standard muffin tin with cooking spray.

2. In a medium bowl, whisk the eggs, milk, maple syrup, vanilla, cinnamon, nutmeg, and salt until very well combined.

3. Add the bread cubes to the egg mixture. Using a spatula, press down to make sure all the bread is soaking. Let sit for 5 minutes.

4. Scoop the bread mixture into the prepared muffin tin, filling the wells all the way to the top.

5. Press the blueberries into the batter (if using). Sprinkle the muffin tops with a pinch of sugar.

6. Bake for 20 minutes, or until the eggs are set. Serve warm with maple syrup. Wrap leftover muffins individually in parchment paper, then plastic wrap and refrigerate for up to 3 days, or freeze for 1 month. Remove the plastic wrap before reheating in the microwave for 30 seconds to 1 minute from frozen.

MAKE IT YOUR OWN

This recipe works with all types of bread, such as Italian, French, or honey wheat bread. Try this recipe with other chopped fruit. You can make regular French toast with this recipe. Instead of cubing the bread, combine the milk and egg mixture and dredge the bread slices in it, soaking both sides. Heat a skillet over medium heat and melt 1 tablespoon of butter. Fry the bread for several minutes on each side until golden brown.

Per Serving (1 muffin): Calories: 114; Fat: 3g; Protein: 5g; Carbohydrates: 17g; Fiber: 1g; Sodium: 65mg; Sugar: 5g

French Toast Roll-Ups

French toast is usually made by dredging bread into an egg and milk mixture and frying it in a skillet. This recipe changes it up a little by flattening the bread, topping it with a spread and fresh berries, and rolling it up before dredging. Try it with the delicious hazelnut spread or make it your own by using other spreads, like cream cheese or nut butters. **SERVES 6**

VEGETARIAN

PREP TIME: 10 MINUTES
COOK TIME: 10 MINUTES

6 slices bread of choice

Hazelnut spread, for topping (like Nutella)

1 cup strawberries, diced

2 large eggs

2 tablespoons heavy (whipping) cream, or milk

½ teaspoon ground cinnamon

Pinch ground nutmeg

Pinch salt

2 tablespoons grass-fed butter

Sugar, for sprinkling

Maple syrup, for serving

1. Put the bread on a work surface. Using a rolling pin, roll the bread flat to resemble tortillas. Cut off the crusts.

2. Spread a generous amount of hazelnut spread on each slice of bread. Sprinkle on the strawberries. Roll the slices and set the rolls aside, seam-side down. The hazelnut spread should hold the edge in place.

3. In a shallow dish, whisk the eggs, heavy cream, cinnamon, nutmeg, and salt until well blended.

4. On a griddle or in a skillet over medium heat, melt the butter.

5. Dredge each bread roll in the egg mixture and place it on the griddle, seam-side down. This will help keep the roll together. Cook for 1 to 2 minutes per side until browned. Remove from the heat and sprinkle sugar on top. Serve hot with maple syrup. Refrigerate leftovers in an airtight container for up to 5 days.

Per Serving: Calories: 213; Fat: 12g; Protein: 7g; Carbohydrates: 21g; Fiber: 3g; Sodium: 216mg; Sugar: 9g

Cinnamon Waffles

Waffles are a quintessential breakfast item. A crisp honeycomb exterior and a fluffy, slightly sweet interior make a perfect combination. You will need a waffle iron to make this recipe, or you can use the batter to make pancakes if you don't have one. This recipe calls for peanut butter to increase the protein content and smashed bananas for sweetness. You can prepare a batch and freeze them for later. When it's time to eat, pop them in the toaster from frozen to reheat. MAKES 8 OR 9 WAFFLES

VEGETARIAN

PREP TIME: 10 MINUTES

COOK TIME: 15 MINUTES

2 cups all-purpose flour, or white whole-wheat flour

2 teaspoons baking powder

1 teaspoon ground cinnamon

½ teaspoon salt

2 ripe bananas

½ cup peanut butter

2 large eggs

1½ cups whole milk

½ teaspoon vanilla extract

1. Heat a waffle iron according to the manufacturer's instructions while you prepare the batter.

2. In a large bowl, whisk the flour, baking powder, cinnamon, and salt.

3. In a medium bowl, mash the bananas. Stir in the peanut butter until well combined. Beat in the eggs and whisk in the milk and vanilla. Pour the wet ingredients into the dry ingredients and stir to combine until the flour mix is well incorporated.

4. Pour ⅓ cup of batter onto each waffle square. Close the iron and cook until done. Most waffle irons indicate when the waffle is done, with adjustable settings to cook to each person's liking. If the waffle iron does not send an alert when done, you will know it's done when there is steam coming out the sides of the waffle iron. Until then, resist the urge to open the iron to check. Repeat until all the batter is used, for about 8 waffles.

INGREDIENT TIP

If you're gluten free, use 1½ cups of almond flour and ¾ cup of brown rice flour in place of the all-purpose flour.

Per Serving (2 waffles): Calories: 502; Fat: 20g; Protein: 20g; Carbohydrates: 66g; Fiber: 4g; Sodium: 454mg; Sugar: 14g

Protein-Packed Banana Pancakes

Traditional pancakes made with refined sugar and flours can give you a sugar rush but then make you crash midmorning. These pancakes substitute banana and honey for sweetness, preventing the sugar crash. Greek yogurt and flaxseed pack protein and fiber for sustained energy. **MAKES 8 PANCAKES**

VEGETARIAN

PREP TIME: 5 MINUTES

COOK TIME: 10 MINUTES

1 banana

¾ cup vanilla Greek yogurt

1 large egg

1 tablespoon local honey

½ cup whole-wheat flour

1 teaspoon baking soda

1 tablespoon ground flaxseed

¼ teaspoon salt

2 tablespoons coconut oil

1. In a medium bowl, smash the banana. Stir in the yogurt, egg, and honey until well combined.

2. Add the flour, baking soda, flaxseed, and salt. Stir until a thick batter forms (a few lumps are okay).

3. Heat a large skillet over medium heat. Add the coconut oil to melt.

4. Using a ¼-cup measure, scoop the batter for 8 pancakes into the hot skillet. Cook for 5 minutes. Using a spatula, flip and cook for 5 minutes more. You can freeze and reheat. Freeze leftover pancakes, with a layer of parchment paper or wax paper between them, in an airtight container. Microwave from frozen for 30 seconds.

THE NIGHT BEFORE

Prepare the batter the night before and refrigerate it in a zip-top bag. In the morning, use scissors to snip a bottom corner of the bag and pipe the batter onto the preheated skillet.

Per Serving (1 pancake): Calories: 110; Fat: 5g; Protein: 3g; Carbohydrates: 14g; Fiber: 1g; Sodium: 193mg; Sugar: 6g

Bacon Cheddar Waffles

Who says waffles can only be sweet? Switch up the routine with these savory waffles filled with bacon and cheese. The waffle iron will melt the cheese into a crisp crust for a satisfying crunch. Top with sautéed spinach and a runny egg, and enjoy this recipe as an occasional and indulgent treat that's filling and packed with protein. MAKES 8 OR 9 WAFFLES

PREP TIME: 10 MINUTES

COOK TIME: 15 MINUTES

For the waffles

1 cup all-purpose flour, or white whole-wheat flour

1 teaspoon baking powder

½ teaspoon salt

½ teaspoon garlic powder

1 cup milk

1 large egg

2 tablespoons grass-fed butter, melted

2 cooked bacon slices, chopped

¼ cup shredded Cheddar cheese, or 1 slice cheese

To make the waffles

1. Preheat the waffle iron according to the manufacturer's instructions.

2. In a medium bowl, whisk the flour, baking powder, salt, and garlic powder.

3. In a liquid measuring cup, whisk the milk, egg, and melted butter. Pour the wet ingredients into the dry ingredients, using a spatula to fold them in. Pour the batter into the waffle maker. Sprinkle with the bacon and cheddar cheese.

4. Close the iron and cook until done. Most waffle irons indicate when the waffle is done, with adjustable settings to cook to each person's liking. If the waffle iron does not send an alert when done, you will know it's done when there is steam coming out the sides of the waffle iron. Until then, resist the urge to open the iron to check. Repeat until all the batter is used, for about 8 waffles.

For the topping

2 tablespoons grass-fed butter, or extra-virgin olive oil

4 cups fresh spinach

4 large eggs

Salt

Freshly ground black pepper

To make the topping

1. In a skillet over medium-high heat, melt the butter. Add the spinach. Cover the skillet with a lid and cook for about 2 minutes to let the spinach begin to wilt.

2. Move the spinach to the side and crack the eggs into the skillet on the other side. You may need to work in batches. Cook the eggs to your desired doneness. Season with salt and pepper.

3. Plate the waffles and top each with the spinach and 1 egg.

THE NIGHT BEFORE

Make a batch of waffles in advance and keep them refrigerated. In the morning, sauté the spinach and fry the egg, as directed, while you reheat the waffles in a toaster.

Per serving: Calories: 438; Fat: 26g; Protein: 20g; Carbohydrates: 32g; Fiber: 2g; Sodium: 567mg; Sugar: 4g

Pancake Dry Mix

Whole-wheat flour gives this recipe its nutritious quality but can be a turn off for some. You can substitute white flour or play around with alternate flours, such as buckwheat and spelt. Make a batch of dry pancake mix, keep it in a jar, and then add melted butter, buttermilk, and syrup the morning of to have homemade pancakes in just 10 minutes. You can double or triple the recipe and store it so you are always ready for a pancake-craving emergency. **MAKES 12 PANCAKES**

VEGETARIAN

PREP TIME: 5 MINUTES

COOK TIME: 10 MINUTES

1 cup whole-wheat flour

1 teaspoon baking powder

½ teaspoon baking soda

¼ teaspoon salt

2 large eggs

1 tablespoon pure
  maple syrup, plus more
  for serving

¾ to 1 cup buttermilk
  (see tip)

2 tablespoons
  grass-fed butter

1. In a medium bowl, whisk the flour, baking powder, baking soda, and salt until evenly combined. Transfer to a clean glass jar, seal, and store for later use, or continue to prepare the pancakes.

2. Pour the dry ingredients into a large bowl. Add the eggs, maple syrup, and buttermilk, starting with ¾ cup. Whisk to break up the eggs and gently stir the ingredients to combine. If you need more liquid, add the remaining ¼ cup of buttermilk to achieve the desired consistency. The ideal consistency for fluffy pancakes is a slightly thick, still lumpy, cakey batter that will still spread slightly when poured into the skillet.

3. Heat a skillet over medium-high heat.

4. Reduce the heat to medium and add the butter to melt.

5. Scoop ¼ cup of batter into the skillet and repeat if you have more room. Cook for 2 to 3 minutes, or until small bubbles appear on the uncooked surface. Using a spatula, flip the pancake and cook for 2 to 3 minutes more, or until browned and cooked through. Serve hot with maple syrup.

COOKING HACK

No buttermilk? No problem. For every 1 cup of buttermilk needed, combine 1 cup of milk and 1 teaspoon of freshly squeezed lemon juice in a liquid measuring cup. Stir and let sit for 5 minutes. The milk will start to curdle. Voilà: buttermilk!

THE NIGHT BEFORE

Another way to ramp up the nutrition content of pancakes is to soak the flour in buttermilk for 12 to 24 hours to ferment it. Fermented foods promote gut health.

Per Serving (1 pancake): Calories: 78; Fat: 3g; Protein: 3g; Carbohydrates: 10g; Fiber: 0g; Sodium: 148mg; Sugar: 2g

Crêpe Shells

Making crêpes can be a bit intimidating unless you use the right pan and master the technique. To remove some of the mystery, think of them as thin pancakes cooked quickly in a hot pan. They can be used to make breakfast and wrap leftovers, and there really is no limit to the number of filling combinations to try with them. Make a batch and store them in the freezer or refrigerator to have ready any time. **MAKES 10 SHELLS**

VEGETARIAN

PREP TIME: 5 MINUTES

COOK TIME: 20 MINUTES

1 cup whole-wheat flour

1 cup milk

3 large eggs

¼ cup water

1 tablespoon grass-fed butter, melted

¼ teaspoon salt

1 tablespoon local honey (optional)

½ teaspoon vanilla extract (optional)

1 tablespoon grass-fed butter, unmelted

1. In a food processor or blender, combine the flour, milk, eggs, water, melted butter, salt, and honey and vanilla (if using for a sweeter version). Pulse until well combined. The batter should look runny.

2. Heat a 10-inch skillet over medium heat. Add the unmelted butter to the pan and melt, swirling the pan off the heat to coat the bottom. Make sure the butter does not burn.

3. Use a ¼-cup measure, pour the batter into the heated pan. Lift the pan and use your wrist to swirl the pan gently so the runny batter covers the entire bottom surface and forms a circular shape. If there isn't enough to cover the bottom, add a bit more batter. Let cook for 1 minute. Using a spatula, gently flip the crêpe and cook the other side for 1 minute more.

4. Make a batch and refrigerate or freeze them, wrapped in plastic wrap, in an airtight container for later use. Put a layer of wax paper between the crêpes to prevent them from sticking. Thaw or heat slightly before using or the shells will break. They will keep, refrigerated for up to 5 days, or frozen, for 1 month.

Per Serving (1 crêpe): Calories: 97; Fat: 4g; Protein: 4g; Carbohydrates: 11g; Fiber: 0g; Sodium: 105mg; Sugar: 1g

Per Serving (1 sweetened crêpe, with vanilla and honey): Calories: 167; Fat: 4g; Protein: 4g; Carbohydrates: 29g; Fiber: 0g; Sodium: 105mg; Sugar: 19g

Crêpe Filling

Filled crêpes can be a decadent dessert or a nutritious breakfast, depending on your filling choices. In this recipe, you will find three different fillings, but the possibilities are endless. SERVES 1

GLUTEN FREE

VEGETARIAN

SUPER-RUSHED

PREP TIME: 2 MINUTES

COOK TIME: 5 MINUTES

For a savory filling

1 mushroom, diced

Small fistful fresh
    spinach, stemmed

1 large egg

1 tablespoon sour cream

Salt

Freshly ground
    black pepper

Feta cheese, for sprinkling

For a sweet filling

1 tablespoon nut butter,
    such as almond or peanut

½ banana, sliced

Dark chocolate sauce, for
    drizzling

For a creamy filling

¼ cup plain Greek yogurt

2 strawberries, hulled
    and sliced

2 tablespoons Homemade
    Granola (page 32), or
    store-bought granola

Local honey, for drizzling

To make the savory filling

1. In a small skillet over medium-high heat, sauté the mushroom and spinach for about 5 minutes until soft.

2. Meanwhile, in a small bowl, whisk the egg and sour cream. Pour the egg over the veggies. Cook, stirring, until egg is scrambled to your desired doneness. Season with salt and pepper and fill the crêpe shell. Sprinkle feta cheese on top and fold the crêpe to serve.

To make the sweet filling

Place a crêpe shell on a work surface. Spread the nut butter on the shell, dot with the banana slices, and drizzle with chocolate sauce. Fold the crêpe and drizzle with more chocolate, if desired.

To make the creamy filling

Place a crêpe shell on a work surface. Spread the yogurt on the shell. Top with the strawberries and granola and drizzle with honey.

Per Serving (1 crêpe with savory filling): Calories: 121; Fat: 9g; Protein: 8g; Carbohydrates: 2g; Fiber: 1g; Sodium: 186mg; Sugar: 1g

Per Serving (1 crêpe with sweet filling): Calories: 197; Fat: 9g; Protein: 5g; Carbohydrates: 29g; Fiber: 3g; Sodium: 82mg; Sugar: 20g

Per Serving (1 crêpe with creamy filling): Calories: 104; Fat: 8g; Protein: 11g; Carbohydrates: 26g; Fiber: 3g; Sodium: 33mg; Sugar: 15g

Strawberry Scones,

CHAPTER 9

Muffins, Breads, and Bars

Processed breads and muffins make subpar breakfast items, but baking them at home means you know exactly what is going into them and you can create nutrient-rich options. In this chapter, you will find cookies, muffins, and other breakfast pastries that utilize wheat flour, add protein and other vitamins and minerals, and, when baking, will fill your home with a lovely aroma.

Breakfast Cookies

Sometimes you just need a cookie for breakfast. Biting into this chewy oatmeal cookie will satisfy any sweet tooth, but it doesn't contain any added processed sugar. The flavors of banana and almond butter pair well with a side of vanilla yogurt. If you would like a bit of a crunch, add nuts or seeds to the dough. **MAKES 12 COOKIES**

DAIRY FREE

VEGAN

PREP TIME: 7 MINUTES

COOK TIME: 12 MINUTES

1 banana

½ cup almond butter

½ cup old-fashioned oats

2 tablespoons all-purpose flour or white whole-wheat flour

½ teaspoon baking soda

½ teaspoon sea salt

½ cup dark chocolate chips

1. Preheat the oven to 350°F. Line a baking sheet with parchment paper or a silicone baking mat.

2. In a medium bowl, using the back of a fork, smash the banana and stir in the almond butter until well combined.

3. In a small bowl, stir together the oats, flour, baking soda, and salt until well mixed. Pour the dry ingredients into the banana mixture and stir until combined. Stir in the chocolate chips. Using a tablespoon, scoop portions onto the prepared baking sheet.

4. Bake for 10 to 12 minutes until slightly brown. Let cool. Keep refrigerated in an airtight container for up to 1 week.

Per Serving (1 cookie): Calories: 115; Fat: 8g; Protein: 3g; Carbohydrates: 11g; Fiber: 1g; Sodium: 177mg; Sugar: 4g

Spiced Pumpkin Muffins

This recipe is fall in a muffin; think pumpkin spice meets your favorite breakfast pastry. Pair it with a warm cup of coffee or tea, and there's no way to have a bad day. Made with maple syrup instead of sugar and filled with vitamins and antioxidants from pumpkin, this treat is actually good for you. MAKES 12 MUFFINS

DAIRY FREE

VEGETARIAN

PREP TIME: 8 MINUTES

COOK TIME: 20 MINUTES

Nonstick cooking spray

2 cups all-purpose flour, or white whole-wheat flour

½ cup packed light brown sugar

2 teaspoons ground cinnamon

1 teaspoon baking soda

½ teaspoon salt

¼ teaspoon ground nutmeg

¼ teaspoon ground cloves

1 (15-ounce) can pumpkin purée

¾ cup pure maple syrup

½ cup coconut oil

2 large eggs

1 teaspoon vanilla extract

1. Preheat the oven to 375°F. Lightly coat a standard muffin tin with cooking spray.

2. In a large bowl, whisk the flour, brown sugar, cinnamon, baking soda, salt, nutmeg, and cloves until combined.

3. In a medium bowl, whisk the pumpkin, maple syrup, coconut oil, eggs, and vanilla until well combined. Pour the wet ingredients into the dry ingredients and gently stir until just combined. Fill the prepared muffin tin with the batter, filling each well about three-quarters full.

4. Bake for 18 to 20 minutes. Test for doneness by gently pressing a finger on the top of a muffin. If it bounces back, it is done. Transfer the muffins to a wire rack to cool.

5. Store leftovers in in airtight container, lined with paper towels, at room temperature for 4 days.

VARIATION TIP

This recipe makes 12 standard-size muffins. If you prefer to make bite-size mini muffins, this recipe will make 24 mini muffins. Reduce the bake time to 15 to 18 minutes.

Per Serving (1 muffin): Calories: 253; Fat: 10g; Protein: 4g; Carbohydrates: 38g; Fiber: 2g; Sodium: 217mg; Sugar: 19g

Blueberry Muffins

A blueberry muffin has long been heralded as a delicious morning treat. Making them from scratch ensures both the deliciousness and nutrition. Load these muffins with antioxidant-rich blueberries. Sugar and oats sprinkled on top add a nice crunch to round out the perfectly fluffy muffin. **MAKES 12 MUFFINS**

VEGETARIAN

PREP TIME: 10 MINUTES

COOK TIME: 30 MINUTES

Nonstick cooking spray

8 tablespoons (1 stick) grass-fed butter, at room temperature

1¼ cups plus 2 teaspoons sugar, divided

2 large eggs

1 teaspoon vanilla extract

1 cup whole-wheat flour

1 cup all-purpose flour, or white whole-wheat flour

2 teaspoons baking powder

½ teaspoon salt

½ cup milk

2 cups fresh blueberries, picked over, and divided

3 teaspoons old-fashioned oats

1. Preheat the oven to 375°F. Lightly coat a standard muffin tin with cooking spray.

2. In a medium bowl, using a handheld electric mixer, cream together the butter and 1¼ cups of sugar until light and fluffy. Add the eggs and beat until well combined. Stir in the vanilla.

3. In another medium bowl, stir together whole-wheat and all-purpose flours, baking powder, and salt. Mixing gently, slowly pour the dry ingredients into the sugar mixture, alternating with the milk. Mix until combined.

4. Crush 1 cup of blueberries with the back of a fork and mix them into the batter. Fold in the remaining 1 cup of blueberries. Fill the prepared muffin tin with the batter.

5. Sprinkle the tops of each muffin with the remaining 2 teaspoons of sugar and the oats.

6. Bake for 25 to 30 minutes, or until a toothpick inserted into the center comes out clean. Let cool.

LOVE YOUR LEFTOVERS

Fresh muffins are a bit trickier to store than their store-bought counterparts. Rather than becoming stale, the moisture will leak out of the muffin and make the surface sticky and damp. It is best to store homemade muffins in an airtight container lined with paper towels. If the muffins contain cream cheese or cheese, refrigerate the container; otherwise, storing them on the counter is fine.

MAKE IT HEALTHIER

If you are concerned about the refined sugar content in this muffin, there are a few options. You can use organic coconut sugar and replace the granulated sugar in a 1:1 ratio. Or, replace the sugar with ¾ cup of pure maple syrup.

Per Serving (1 muffin): Calories: 251; Fat: 9g; Protein: 4g; Carbohydrates: 41g; Fiber: 2g; Sodium: 115mg; Sugar: 24g

High-Fiber Carrot Cake Muffins

Do you love juicing but wonder what you can do with the leftover pulp? Why not use the fibrous remains for a morning muffin? This muffin is delicious, like carrot cake but without the added sugar. In the morning, heat a muffin in the microwave and spread on a creamy layer of cream cheese or warm butter. **MAKES 20 MUFFINS**

VEGETARIAN

PREP TIME: 10 MINUTES
BAKE TIME: 20 MINUTES

Nonstick cooking spray
1 ripe banana
4 large eggs
½ cup plain Greek yogurt
½ cup applesauce, or
  Seasonal Fruit Compote
  (page 28)
½ cup pure maple syrup
¼ cup local honey
1½ cups whole-wheat flour
¼ cup ground flaxseed
2 teaspoons baking powder
2 teaspoons baking soda
2 teaspoons ground
  cinnamon
1 teaspoon ground nutmeg
½ teaspoon salt
2 cups juicer pulp (from
  Ginger Carrot Juice,
  page 19, or see cooking
  hack tip, following)
½ cup chopped pecans, or
  walnuts (optional)
Old-fashioned oats, for
  sprinkling (optional)

1. Preheat the oven to 350°F. Coat 2 standard muffin tins (20 wells total) with cooking spray.

2. In the bowl of a stand mixer fitted with the paddle attachment, or in a large bowl and using a hand-held electric mixer, smash the banana and beat in the eggs until well combined. Blend in the yogurt, applesauce, maple syrup, and honey.

3. In a medium bowl, whisk the flour, flaxseed, baking powder, baking soda, cinnamon, nutmeg, and salt until well combined. Stir in the juicer pulp.

4. Fold the dry ingredients into the wet ingredients and stir until just combined.

5. Stir in the pecans (if using). Fill the muffin tins with the batter, each about two-thirds full. If you'd like a little texture on top, sprinkle the muffins with the oats.

6. Bake for 20 minutes. Test for doneness by gently pressing a finger on the top of a muffin. If it bounces back, it is done.

COOKING HACK

If you do not have pulp to use, replace it with 1 carrot, shredded; ½ apple, shredded; and the grated zest of ½ orange.

LOVE YOUR LEFTOVERS

To store leftovers, it is important to let the muffins cool completely. To prevent sad, soggy muffins, line an airtight container with paper towels and put the muffins on top; then, place a paper towel on top of muffins and secure the lid. Store on the counter at room temperature for several days. The paper towels help absorb excess moisture. If you would like to store for longer than 4 days, wrap the muffins individually in plastic wrap and freeze them. Let them thaw at room temperature, or rewarm for 30 seconds in the microwave.

Per Serving (1 muffin): Calories: 105; Fat: 2g; Protein: 3g; Carbohydrates: 20g; Fiber: 1g; Sodium: 209mg; Sugar: 10g

PB Protein Bites

If eating these is wrong, I don't want to be right. They are addictive but surprisingly filling, so enjoy 2 to 3 balls, and you are good to go. These no-bake bites are a fantastic source of protein and fiber to start your day with the fuel you need to sustain your morning activities. MAKES 12 BITES

GLUTEN FREE

VEGETARIAN

PREP TIME: 15 MINUTES

1 cup old-fashioned oats

½ cup peanut butter

½ cup dark chocolate chips

⅓ cup local honey

¼ cup ground flaxseed

1 tablespoon chia seeds

1. In a food processor, combine the oats, peanut butter, chocolate chips, honey, flaxseed, and chia seeds. Process until a dough-like consistency is reached.

2. By the heaping tablespoonful, roll the mixture into balls. Refrigerate in an airtight container for up to 1 week (bet they won't last that long!).

MAKE IT AHEAD

Make a batch, or even double the recipe, to make these bites for the upcoming week. Keep refrigerated in an airtight container until you are ready to eat. I like to package 2 or 3 bites together in resealable to-go bags to make it easy to grab and go in the morning.

Per Serving (2 or 3 bites): Calories: 166; Fat: 9g; Protein: 5g; Carbohydrates: 20g; Fiber: 3g; Sodium: 52mg; Sugar: 12g

Coconut Cacao Balls

According to historic accounts, the Aztecs and Mayans believed cacao to be a gift from their gods. Cacao is the purest form of chocolate, and when you hear that chocolate is good for you, it's raw cacao they're talking about. It is high in antioxidants and other health-boosting qualities. When mixed with the high-quality fat of cashews, this ball tosses a powerhouse of good energy into your breakfast routine. MAKES 12 BALLS

DAIRY FREE

GLUTEN FREE

VEGETARIAN

PREP TIME: 10 MINUTES

CHILL TIME: 30 MINUTES

FREEZING TIME:

25 MINUTES

For the base

2 cups raw cashews

1 cup shredded coconut

¾ cup cacao powder

½ cup cacao nibs

¼ cup pure maple syrup

1 teaspoon vanilla extract

1 teaspoon salt

For the topping

1 cup coconut oil

½ cup pure maple syrup

½ cup cacao powder

1 teaspoon salt

1 teaspoon vanilla extract

To make the base

1. In a food processor, combine the cashews and coconut. Process for 10 to 15 seconds.

2. Add the cacao powder, cacao nibs, maple syrup, vanilla, and salt. Process until well combined and a paste forms. Refrigerate to chill for 30 minutes.

3. With your hands, roll the chilled mixture into truffle-size balls. Place the balls on a plate and put them in the freezer for 20 minutes to set.

To make the topping

In a food processor or blender, combine the coconut oil, maple syrup, cacao powder, salt, and vanilla. Blend until mixed. Transfer to a bowl.

To assemble the balls

1. Using a fork, spear a truffle ball. Dip the ball into the topping mix, swirling to cover it completely. Put the ball on the chilled plate and repeat with the remaining balls. When done, put the plate with the covered balls back in the freezer for about 5 minutes to set.

2. Refrigerate in an airtight container for up 1 week (or as long as they last, which isn't long in my house).

Per Serving (1 ball): Calories: 422; Fat: 35g; Protein: 6g; Carbohydrates: 30g; Fiber: 7g; Sodium: 295mg; Sugar: 13g

Sweet Potato Breakfast Biscuits

Biscuits and gravy are a traditional Southern breakfast, but no one is calling them healthy. This recipe changes things up a bit and adds nutrients with the use of mashed sweet potato for an infusion of fiber. These drop biscuits are easy to make and delicious to eat. Add a scrambled egg and maple bacon for a tasty breakfast sandwich. **MAKES 12 TO 15 BISCUITS**

VEGETARIAN

PREP TIME: 10 MINUTES

COOK TIME: 19 MINUTES

5 tablespoons plus 1 teaspoon grass-fed butter

1 large sweet potato

2 cups all-purpose flour, or white whole-wheat flour

1 tablespoon sugar

1 tablespoon baking powder

1 teaspoon ground cinnamon

½ teaspoon salt

1 cup buttermilk, chilled (see cooking hack tip, following)

1. Preheat the oven to 425°F. Line a baking sheet with parchment paper and set aside.

2. Put the butter in the freezer to quick chill.

3. Using a fork, poke holes in the sweet potato. Microwave the sweet potato for 7 minutes to soften. Let cool. Peel off the skin and discard it. Put the sweet potato in a small bowl and smash it with a potato masher. If you prefer a smoother texture, put the sweet potato into a food processor and purée until smooth. Put the mashed sweet potato in the freezer to quick chill while you work through the rest of the steps.

4. In a medium bowl, whisk the flour, sugar, baking powder, cinnamon, and salt until well mixed.

5. Using a box grater, grate the cold butter into the flour mixture. Using 2 knives or a pastry blender, cut the butter into the flour. The mixture should look like coarse sand.

6. In a small bowl, stir together the mashed sweet potato and buttermilk. Pour the wet mixture into the flour and fold it in until just combined. Using a ⅓-cup measure, scoop the biscuit batter and drop it onto the prepared baking sheet, leaving 2 inches between each biscuit.

7. Bake for 10 to 12 minutes, until the outer surface is firm. Remove from the oven and let cool. Slice, spread with butter if you like, and serve warm or use to make a sandwich.

COOKING HACK

No buttermilk? No problem. For every 1 cup of buttermilk needed, combine 1 cup of milk and 1 teaspoon of freshly squeezed lemon juice in a liquid measuring cup. Stir and let sit for 5 minutes. The milk will start to curdle. Voilà: buttermilk!

Per Serving (1 biscuit): Calories: 144; Fat: 6g; Protein: 3g; Carbohydrates: 21g; Fiber: 1g; Sodium: 162mg; Sugar: 2g

Strawberry Scones

The word "scone" originated from the Dutch and means "beautiful bread." These little wedges of beautifully baked goodness are filled with juicy red strawberries and make a satisfying breakfast bite paired with a warm cup of coffee or tea. You can make the dough ahead and bake it in the morning for a special breakfast treat. It is very important to keep the butter cold when making the scones. This helps create little air pockets in the pastry to make it fluffy. MAKES 8 SCONES

VEGETARIAN

PREP TIME: 10 MINUTES

COOK TIME: 15 MINUTES

2 large eggs

1 tablespoon plus ¼ cup whole milk, divided

¼ cup buttermilk (see cooking hack tip, following)

1 teaspoon vanilla extract

2 cups white whole-wheat flour, plus more for dusting

⅓ cup plus 1 tablespoon sugar, divided

2 teaspoons baking powder

¼ teaspoon salt

6 tablespoons cold grass-fed butter, cut into 1-inch pieces and kept chilled

⅔ cup chopped fresh or frozen strawberries

1. Preheat the oven to 375°F. Line a baking sheet with parchment paper.

2. In a small bowl, beat 1 egg with 1 tablespoon of milk and set aside.

3. In a medium bowl, whisk the remaining egg, remaining ¼ cup of milk, the buttermilk, and vanilla until blended.

4. In a food processor, combine the flour, ⅓ cup of sugar, baking powder, and salt. Pulse until blended.

5. Add the cold butter and pulse for about 10 seconds until the mixture resembles coarse cornmeal. Transfer the mixture to a large bowl and make a well in center.

6. Add the buttermilk mixture into the well and stir, incorporating the liquid into the dry ingredients, until a batter forms with moist lumps.

7. Carefully stir in the strawberries.

8. Lightly flour a work surface and transfer the dough to it. Gently knead the dough until it comes together and is smooth, about 10 seconds. Pat the dough into a 7-inch circle about 1 inch thick. Cut the circle into 8 wedges. Brush off any excess flour with a pastry brush. Place the wedges on the prepared baking sheet and brush their tops with the egg and milk glaze. Sprinkle the remaining 1 tablespoon of sugar on top.

9. Bake for about 15 minutes until lightly browned. Transfer the scones to a wire rack. Serve warm or at room temperature.

COOKING HACK

No buttermilk? No problem. For every 1 cup of buttermilk needed, combine 1 cup of milk and 1 teaspoon of freshly squeezed lemon juice in a liquid measuring cup. Stir and let sit for 5 minutes. The milk will start to curdle. Voilà: buttermilk!

THE NIGHT BEFORE

Make the dough in advance and refrigerate (without the egg wash and sugar sprinkle) for up to 2 days before you are ready to bake. That way, you can have warm scones while still in your pajamas. You can also freeze the dough and bake it without thawing. Simply remove the dough while the oven is preheating, put it on a parchment-lined baking sheet, brush with the egg wash glaze, and sprinkle sugar on top. Bake as directed. Keep an eye on the scones toward the end of the cooking time as you may need to add a few minutes.

Per Serving (1 scone): Calories: 203; Fat: 9g; Protein: 5g; Carbohydrates: 29g; Fiber: 3g; Sodium: 82mg; Sugar: 12g

Slow Cooker Raisin Bran Loaf

A slow cooker is not just used for making dinner; it can also be used to make deliciously moist loaves of morning bread. This recipe uses bran-flake cereal and raisins, so it is like a bran muffin in loaf form. It is subtly sweet and filled with fiber. Slice and serve with warm butter for a simple breakfast. **SERVES 12**

VEGETARIAN

PREP TIME: 20 MINUTES
COOK TIME: 3 HOURS,
15 MINUTES

Nonstick cooking spray
1¾ cups buttermilk
  (see cooking hack tip,
  following)
½ cup local honey
¼ cup coconut oil
1 large egg
2 cups bran cereal
1 cup whole-wheat flour
1 cup all-purpose flour, or
  white whole-wheat flour
2 teaspoons baking powder
1 teaspoon baking soda
¾ teaspoon salt
½ teaspoon cinnamon
1 cup raisins
½ cup chopped pecans
2 tablespoons
  old-fashioned oats

1. Coat a 6-quart glass baking dish (or round bowl) with cooking spray. It should fit inside your slow cooker with clearance all around.

2. In a large bowl, whisk the buttermilk, honey, coconut oil, and egg until blended. Pour in the bran cereal and let sit for 10 to 15 minutes to soften.

3. Stir in the whole-wheat and all-purpose flours, the baking powder, baking soda, salt, and cinnamon until well combined. Fold in the raisins and pecans. Pour the batter into the prepared baking dish. Sprinkle on the oats. Cover the dish with 2 layers of foil and make sure it is securely wrapped. Place the dish into a slow cooker. Carefully pour water into the cooker until it reaches halfway up the sides of the baking dish.

4. Cover the cooker and cook on high heat for 3 hours.

5. After 3 hours, carefully remove the baking dish and the foil. Press down gently on the loaf; if it springs back, it is done. If it needs to cook longer, re-cover it with the foil, return it to the slow cooker, and cook for 15 minutes more. When done, transfer to a wire rack to cool.

Toss the raisins in flour to prevent them from sinking to the bottom of the baking dish.

No buttermilk? No problem. For every 1 cup of buttermilk needed, combine 1 cup of milk and 1 teaspoon of freshly squeezed lemon juice in a liquid measuring cup. Stir and let sit for 5 minutes. The milk will start to curdle. Voilà: buttermilk!

MAKE IT HEALTHIER

If you want to cut down on the sugar, use unsweetened or no-added-sugar raisins.

Per Serving: Calories: 249; Fat: 8g; Protein: 7g; Carbohydrates: 43g; Fiber: 6g; Sodium: 287mg; Sugar: 20g

Dried Fruit Bars

These nutrient-filled bars are chewy and chock-full of clean fuel from dried fruit and nuts. This is great to make year-round, especially when fresh fruit is not in season. This recipe uses pecans, walnuts, figs, and dates, but the options for other flavors are endless; try dried cranberries, dates, and pistachios, or apricots and almonds. MAKES 20 BARS

DAIRY FREE

GLUTEN FREE

VEGETARIAN

PREP TIME: 10 MINUTES

FREEZING TIME:

20 MINUTES

Nonstick cooking spray

1 cup pecans

1 cup walnuts

2 cups dried figs

¼ cup pitted dates

2 teaspoons local honey

1 teaspoon vanilla extract

Pinch salt

1. Lightly coat a 9-by-10-inch glass baking dish with cooking spray and set aside.

2. In a food processor or blender, pulse the pecans and walnuts several times to begin to chop them up.

3. Add the figs, dates, honey, vanilla, and salt. Blend until the dried fruit becomes a paste to hold everything together.

4. Press the mixture into the prepared baking dish and put it into the freezer to chill for 15 to 20 minutes. Cut into small bars. Refrigerate in an airtight container for up to 2 weeks.

VARIATION TIP

I know I said the flavor combinations are endless—here is another one of my favorites: 1 cup of pecans, 1 cup of almonds, 1 cup of dried apricots, 1 cup of raisins, ¼ cup of pitted dates, 1 teaspoon of vanilla extract, 2 teaspoons of honey, and a pinch of salt. Delicious!

Per Serving (1 bar): Calories: 132; Fat: 8g; Protein: 2g; Carbohydrates: 17g; Fiber: 3g; Sodium: 10mg; Sugar: 12g

Measurement Conversions

	US STANDARD	US STANDARD (OUNCES)	METRIC (APPROXIMATE)
VOLUME EQUIVALENTS (LIQUID)	2 tablespoons	1 fl. oz.	30 mL
	¼ cup	2 fl. oz.	60 mL
	½ cup	4 fl. oz.	120 mL
	1 cup	8 fl. oz.	240 mL
	1 ½ cups	12 fl. oz.	355 mL
	2 cups or 1 pint	16 fl. oz.	475 mL
	4 cups or 1 quart	32 fl. oz.	1 L
	1 gallon	128 fl. oz.	4 L
VOLUME EQUIVALENTS (DRY)	⅛ teaspoon	———	0.5 mL
	¼ teaspoon	———	1 mL
	½ teaspoon	———	2 mL
	¾ teaspoon	———	4 mL
	1 teaspoon	———	5 mL
	1 tablespoon	———	15 mL
	¼ cup	———	59 mL
	⅓ cup	———	79 mL
	½ cup	———	118 mL
	⅔ cup	———	156 mL
	¾ cup	———	177 mL
	1 cup	———	235 mL
	2 cups or 1 pint	———	475 mL
	3 cups	———	700 mL
	4 cups or 1 quart	———	1 L
	½ gallon	———	2 L
	1 gallon	———	4 L
WEIGHT EQUIVALENTS	½ ounce	———	15 g
	1 ounce	———	30 g
	2 ounces	———	60 g
	4 ounces	———	115 g
	8 ounces	———	225 g
	12 ounces	———	340 g
	16 ounces or 1 pound	———	455 g

	FAHRENHEIT (F)	CELSIUS (C) (APPROXIMATE)
OVEN TEMPERATURES	250°F	120°F
	300°F	150°C
	325°F	180°C
	375°F	190°C
	400°F	200°C
	425°F	220°C
	450°F	230°C

Index

Acknowledgments

This book is a culmination of favorite recipes I have used and taught over the years. Food and how we incorporate it into our lives has always been fascinating to me. My love affair with breakfast is long standing but as a business owner who also runs a household with two small children, large elaborate breakfasts become a weekend treat. In an effort to feed my family healthy meals in the morning that don't require long hours in the kitchen but something more than a bowl of cereal, I've developed certain hacks over the years. This book is meant to share these with you in hopes it will help to make your life easier as well.

First, I would like to thank my family, Chris, Alexandria, and Caroline, for always being my rocks as well as my guinea pigs, willing to try what I make, even, if at times, it is a "Chef Shayna fail" and, more importantly, for giving grace when I hide behind a computer while writing and editing in the midst of a messy kitchen.

My mom, who, although she didn't know it, started my passion for food and sharing it with others, as she ran a successful restaurant and let me watch from behind the hostess stand and my dad who showed me how to be unapologetic about pursuing my passions. To my (not so) little brother, for being my biggest cheerleader and supporter.

My students, who have also been my greatest teachers. Always asking questions and inquiring about recipes and food that force me to think a bit longer about my methods in the kitchen. It allows me to gain a better understanding of the struggles hindering people from getting into the kitchen, making meals, and gathering around the table, so we may address them and find solutions with practical tips and tricks.

Last, but not least, my partner in crime in the kitchen, Denise, who has been there through the ups, downs, and everything in between.

About the Author

Shayna Telesmanic lives in California's Central Valley with her husband and two children. She pours her cooking expertise into teaching weekly classes, leading workshops, developing educational programs, and hosting private events. She's also run a cooking school for over a decade and has a weekly segment on Fresno's ABC 30.

Shayna's passion is to simplify cooking for families, take the mystery out of the kitchen, and help people fall in love with cooking healthily. It's something she's had personal experience with. After she had her oldest daughter, she developed a workshop called Supper Club as a way to create community, commiserate, and laugh, all while getting a very crucial part of life done: putting dinner on the table.

CPSIA information can be obtained
at www.ICGtesting.com
Printed in the USA
LVHW071107201219
641177LV00005B/8/P

9 781641 528900